SpringerBriefs in Economics

For further volumes:
http://www.springer.com/series/8876

Carol Yeh-Yun Lin · Leif Edvinsson
Jeffrey Chen · Tord Beding

National Intellectual Capital and the Financial Crisis in Israel, Jordan, South Africa, and Turkey

Springer

Carol Yeh-Yun Lin
Department of Business Administration
National Chengchi University
Taipei
Taiwan

Leif Edvinsson
Universal Networking Intellectual Capital
Norrtälje
Sweden

Jeffrey Chen
Accenture
Chicago, IL
USA

Tord Beding
TC-Growth AB
Karlstad
Sweden

ISSN 2191-5504 ISSN 2191-5512 (electronic)
ISBN 978-1-4614-7980-2 ISBN 978-1-4614-7981-9 (eBook)
DOI 10.1007/978-1-4614-7981-9
Springer New York Heidelberg Dordrecht London

Library of Congress Control Number: 2013940090

Printed on acid-free paper

Springer is part of Springer Science+Business Media (www.springer.com)

Foreword I

The economic crisis is a consequence of many parallel factors which are all related to globalization and digitalization. My main concern, assessing this in more detail from the European perspective, is that revolutionary global forces have not been taken early nor seriously enough by most national and regional decision makers. The Heads of European States and Governments have once again recalled the importance of fiscal consolidation, structural reform, and targeted investment to put Europe back on the path of smart, sustainable, and inclusive growth. The main question is how capable and ready are the national governments to tackling the complex and manifold issues of crises and to renewing even radically many of our public and private structures and processes.

The first basic requirement is that all the European Union Member States remain fully committed to taking the actions required at the national level to achieve the objectives of the Europe 2020 Strategy. The second basic requirement is that the national and regional governments, as well as people, are ready for radical changes. This booklet, and the other 11 booklets by the experienced authors, focus on National intellectual capital (NIC) and give necessary insights and facts for us the readers and especially for our in-depth systemic thinking of the interrelationships of NIC and economic recovery.

How should the national and regional decision makers tackle the existing knowledge of intangible capital? The focus needs to be more on the bottom-up approach stressing the developments on local and regional levels. I highlight our recent statements by the EU Committee of the Regions. The key priorities are to get more innovations out of research and to encourage mindset change towards open innovation.

The political decision makers are finally aware that the traditional indicators created for and used in industrial production cannot be applied to a knowledge-intensive, turbulent, and innovativeness-based global enterprise environment. Indicators that perceive the intangible dimensions of competitiveness—knowledge capital, innovation knowledge, and anticipation of the future—have been developed around the world, but their use has not yet become established in practice. This booklet accelerates the development and the use of these indicators.

This helps the local and regional, as well as central, governments in taking brave leaps forward on a practical level—giving greater ownership and involving all the stakeholders. This means the need of actions towards increasing the structural and relational capital of regions, both internally in communities of practice and in collaboration with others.

The new generation innovation activities are socially motivated, open, and collectively participated, complex and global by nature. The regions need to move towards open innovation, within a human-centered vision of partnerships between public and private sector actors, with universities playing a crucial role.

Regions should be encouraged to develop regional innovation platforms, which act as demand-based service centres and promote the use of international knowledge to implement the Europe 2020 Strategy, smart specialization and European partnerships according to the interests and needs of regions. For this to happen, we need to apply the new dynamic understanding of regional innovation ecosystems, in which companies, cities, and universities as well as other public and private sector actors (the "Triple Helix") learn to work together in new and creative ways to fully harness their innovative potential.

New innovative practices do not come about by themselves. One major potential is the use of public procurement. The renewing of the European wide rules must increase the strategic agility and activities of municipalities and other public operators as creators of new solutions. Especially, the execution of pre-commercial procurement should be reinforced even more in combination with open innovation to speed up the green knowledge society development, i.e., for common re-usable solutions in creating the infrastructures and services modern real-world innovation ecosystems are built upon. Conditions must be created that also allow for extensive development projects which address complex societal challenges and which take the form of risk-taking consortia.

One of our working instruments within the Committee of the Regions is the Europe 2020 Monitoring Platform, which broadly reviews and reflects the opinions and decisions on regional level all around Europe. It gives a flavor of cultural and other socio-economic differences inside the EU. This brings an important perspective to the intellectual capital, namely the values and attitudes needed for citizens supporting policymakers on appropriate long-term investments and policies.

Emphasizing the importance of these issues, decision makers in all countries and regions worldwide need a deep and broad understanding of the critical success factors affecting the NIC. With all the facts and frames for thinking this booklet gives a valuable insight in today's challenges.

Markku Markkula
Advisor to the Aalto University Presidents
Member of the EU Committee of the Regions
Former Member of the Parliament of Finland

Foreword II

Financial crisis—words very much heard today. What is all this about, actually, and how to get a grip on what we experience today? The booklet gives an important insight on the factors affecting competitiveness and productivity in modern knowledge society. We need to see behind the obvious, and we need to have increasingly "qualified guesses" as the character of the society and industry has fundamentally changed.

What is very important to notice is the shift towards intangible value creation beyond the deterministic phenomena we saw very clearly in the industrial era. Cost drivers were the important ones throughout the industry. Mass production, bigger is better; very traditional productivity factors, was the mantra.

However, the production picture is changing. Increasingly value is created by the intangibles, often services related to the tangible components, and even totally in immaterial value creation, where perceptions and expectations determine the market value of the "extended product". We also see rapid change in organizational forms, we see new type of entrepreneurship growing besides the traditional industry clusters, we see smart specialization of regions and countries.

This means also that there will be clearly different and complementary roles of the actors in innovation and value creation ecosystems. Large companies, small ones and even microenterprises together with the public sector are traditionally seen as the active partners in such innovation environments. The real issue in the dynamic markets is, however, that the end users are increasingly to be taken on board as *active subjects* for innovation, and not merely treated as objects, customers. Markets need to be shaped and created in much more dynamic way than ever before. Open innovation beyond cross-licensing includes the societal capital as an important intangible engine for productivity growth. Innovation happens only when the offering is meeting the demand. Otherwise, we can only speak about inventions or ideas.

We need to have a close look at the intellectual capital and the different factors within it when we design our policy approaches. Short-term investments in process capital (infrastructures) and market capital seem to be very important for the manufacturing base as such, but at the same time measures for longer term intellectual capital development and efficiency need to be taken.

Increasingly, important is the *structure* and the open *processes* related to intangible capital and knowledge pools. For sustainable long-term development both the *human capital and renewal capital are crucial*, as they are directly related to the innovation capability of the region. The correlation between these factors and the GDP growth is undisputable. In knowledge intense industries talent is attracting talent, and the connectivity which modern ICT provides makes this talent pool fluid across disciplines, organizations, and geographical settings. It is imperative to modernize the innovation systems enabling the full dynamics needed for success in knowledge intense industries, beyond the traditional boundaries.

Measuring performance of innovation systems becomes increasingly complex due to the mash-up of different disciplines, having new types of actors and interactions between them. Hence, the importance of analysis of the various components of the national intellectual capital (NIC) (and equally on national innovation capability) as done in this booklet cannot be underestimated when making qualified guesses for operational choices to create functioning innovation ecosystems. The only predictable in true innovation is the unpredictability and the surprises. The role of the public sector is to drive strategy and measures enabling the unpredictable, and to catalyze a fluid, seamless and frictionless innovation system to grow, with strong interplay with the surrounding society.

We need to have courage to experiment, to prototype in real-world settings, to have all stakeholders involved to find and remove the friction points of innovation and to achieve sustainable innovation ecosystems for knowledge-intensive products and services.

I wish you interesting reading with this mind opening report.

Bror Salmelin
Advisor, Innovation Systems
European Commission
DG CONNECT

Foreword III

The 2008 global financial crisis hit the whole world with unprecedented speed, causing widespread financial panic. Consumer confidence dropped to the lowest level since the Great Depression. Taiwan, with an export-dependent economy, was seriously impacted by the crisis and the unemployment rate hiked while household consumption levels dropped. At the onset of the financial crisis, Professor Lin was the Dean of Student Affairs here at National Chengchi University in Taipei, Taiwan. She was the dean in charge of financial aid and student loans and thus saw firsthand the direct impact the financial crisis had upon our students. The crisis was so devastating that Professor Lin, along with the university, was compelled to launch several new initiatives to raise money and help students weather the difficult times.

I am very glad that she took this painful experience to heart and set herself upon the task of investigating the impact of the crisis; trying to look into the causes and consequences for policy implications, not only for Taiwan but for an array of 48 countries. In particular, she approaches the crisis from the perspective of "national intellectual capital," which is very important in today's knowledge-driven economy.

Taiwan is an example of a knowledge economy and has enjoyed the fame of being referred to as a "high-tech island." Without an abundance of natural resources, Taiwan's hardworking and highly educated population is the single most precious resource that the island has. Acknowledging the value of such human resources and intellectual capital, we established the Taiwan Intellectual Capital Research Center (TICRC) under my leadership in 2003. Ever since then, Taiwan's government has continuously funded the university to conduct relevant research projects aimed at enhancing the intellectual capital of Taiwan. Having been thus endowed with the responsibility of nourishing future leaders in the public and private sectors, we have focused on building up our strength in innovation, entrepreneurship, and technology management related research and education.

To enhance intellectual capital research, we recently formed a joint team of professors for a four-year project in order to leverage their respective research capabilities. Through this project we hope to provide policy suggestions for the government by exploring the creativity, innovation, and intellectual capital at national, regional, city, and county levels. The goal is to come up with an intangible assets agenda for Taiwan's future sustainability. Professor Lin is an integral member in this research team.

Following her 2011 book *National Intellectual Capital: A Comparison of 40 Countries*, this booklet series is Professor Lin's second attempt at presenting her research, conducted under the sponsorship of TICRC, to international readers. As the Founding Director of TICRC and her President, I am honored to give a brief introduction on the value of this booklet series.

In comparison to her 2011 book, this series increased the number of countries studied to 48 and particularly focuses on the impact of intellectual capital on the 2008 global financial crisis. Rarely has an economic issue been systematically studied from the viewpoint of intangible assets, particularly at such a large scale of 48 countries. The research results show without a doubt that national intellectual capital is indeed an important economic development enhancer. In particular, the fact that countries with higher national intellectual capital experienced faster recoveries from the 2008 financial crisis provides a strong message for the policymakers.

In addition to providing insights into national policy, the booklet also summarizes the background of each country before the crisis, the key events during the crisis, economic development afterwards, and future prospects and challenges. Each volume affords readers a holistic picture of what happened in each country in an efficient manner. The linkage between national intellectual capital and this financial crisis also provides a different perspective of the crisis.

We are happy that Professor Lin continues to share her valuable research results with international readers. I sincerely hope that her insights can garner more attention concerning the benefits of developing national intellectual capital for the well-being of every nation.

Se-Hwa Wu
Professor, Graduate Institute of Technology
and Innovation Management
President, National Chengchi University,
Taipei, Taiwan

Preface I

There are "mounting risks of a breakup of the Euro zone." Such comments are frequent today on how the European leaders are handling the escalating crisis and its potential impact on non-European countries. But few leaders, reporters, or researchers are actually addressing the situation of national intellectual capital (NIC) and its signals. In addition to the financial crisis, is there an emerging NIC crisis as well? Why is it emerging? How should policy makers think about NIC? In what way does it need specific attention? When will the outcome and impact of taken NIC policy steps be realized?

In the midst of the European crisis, there are national interventions to address the issues mentioned above. In leading economical nations the investments going into intangibles now exceeds tangibles, and is positively correlated to income per capita. However, these still do not show up clearly in national mapping as well as policymaking insights. Therefore, the New Club of Paris is focusing the knowledge agenda setting for countries on Societal Innovation (see www.new-club-of-paris.org).

Chairman Ben Bernanke of the U.S. Federal Reserve was addressing some of these same aspects in a key note speech in May 2011 hosted by Georgetown University: http://www.icapitaladvisors.com/2011/05/31/bernanke-on-intangible-capital/. OECD and the World Bank are developing NIC statistics, often based on the model from Corrado-Hultén. Japan has been developing both NIC and Intangible Assets (IA) at METI for some time now. Their research on IC/IA has resulted in a National IA Week with various key stakeholders, such as government agencies, universities, stock exchange, and enterprises. Japan is so far the only country in the world to hold such activities, and they have been doing so for the last eight years. Australia, Singapore, South Korea, and China are currently undertaking various NIC initiatives. Other countries are also becoming more and more aware of NIC, with policy rhetoric centered on innovation, education, R&D, and trade. Despite this, the map for a more justified NIC navigation has been missing.

This booklet highlights NIC development for a number of countries, based on 48 different indicators, aggregated into four major NIC components of human capital, market capital, process capital, and renewal capital. The model here is a refined and verified statistical model in comparison to the Corrado-Hultén model. We call it the L-E-S model after the contributors Lin-Edvinsson-Stahle. Based on a deeper understanding and the timeline pattern it sets forth, this model will add to a better NIC navigation, not to mention knowledge agenda setting for countries.

Upon looking at a global cluster NIC map, it is evident that the top leading countries seem to be small countries, especially Singapore, the Nordic countries, Hong Kong, and Taiwan. For the U.S., Finland, and Sweden around 50 % or more of its economical growth is related to NIC aspects. Sweden, Finland, Switzerland, the U.S., Israel, and Denmark are strongly influenced in its GDP growth by focusing on Renewal Capital.

It might be that we will see a clearer map of the NIC ecosystem and drivers for wealth emerge in the extension of this ongoing unique research of NIC. This booklet will present a NIC map for various clusters of countries. It can be used for benchmarking as well as bench learning for policy prototyping. The starting point is awareness and thinking of NIC, and its drivers for economic results. Based on this more refined navigation, NIC metrics can be presented.

Deeper understanding will emerge from this research, such as the scaling up of limited skilled human capital in one nation by using the globalized broadband technologies for migration and flow of knowledge (such as tele-medicine or mobile banking in Africa). This is also referred to as the IC multiplier. It might also be the way the old British Commonwealth was constructed, but without the IC taxonomy. In modern taxonomy it might be the shaping of NIC alliances for the migration and flow of IC between nations?

Another understanding that might emerge for policymaking is the issue of employment versus unemployment. The critical understanding will be deployment of IC drivers. This will require another networked workforce of value networkers on a global scale, such as volunteering software and apps developers. However such volunteers do not show up in traditional statistics, for the mapping on behalf of policymakers.

On another level there might be a clear gap analyses between nations to support the vision process of a nation. On a deeper level it is also a leadership responsibility to address the gap of NIC positions versus potential positions. Such a gap is in fact a liability to the citizens, to be addressed in due time.

This will take us to the need for the continuous renewal of social systems. The so-called Arab Spring is explained by some as resulting from three drivers: lack of renewal of social systems, Internet, and soccer as cross class interaction space. The lack of social renewal and innovation is most likely critical early warning signals. For Greece, we can see such a tipping point that occurred back in 1999.

On a global scale we might see that the concern for the Euro zone crisis should and can be explained by a deeper and supplementary understanding of National Intellectual Capital, in addition to financial capital. So we need to refine our NIC understanding, NIC mapping, NIC metrics, and NIC organizational constructs into societal innovation for the benefit of wealth creation of subsequent generations.

Leif Edvinsson
The World's First Professor of Intellectual Capital
Chairman and Co-founder of New Club of Paris

Preface II

Our first book *National Intellectual Capital*: *A Comparison of 40 Countries* was published in early 2011, at a time when the 2008 global financial crisis had been declared over yet the European region was still plagued with sovereign debt problems. Before we finalized the book, we were able to retrieve some of our raw data concerning the troubled countries, such as Greece, Iceland, Ireland, Portugal, and Spain. The results of our analysis based on data spanning 1995–2008 revealed some early warning signs of the financial turmoil in those countries. In my preface of that book, I mentioned the warning signs might reveal only the tip of an iceberg. At that time, my co-author, Prof. Edvinsson, and I decided to do a follow up study to trace the development of National Intellectual Capital (NIC) in as many countries as possible, particularly through the lens of the 2008 global financial crisis. This 12 booklet series is the result of that determination.

The 2008 global financial crisis came with unexpected speed and had such a wide-spread effect that surprised many countries far from the epicenter of the initial U.S. sub-prime financial problem, geographically and financially. According to reports, no country was immune from the impact of this financial crisis. Such development clearly signifies how closely connected the world has become and the importance of having a global interdependent view. By reporting what happened during 2005–2010 in 48 major countries throughout the world, this booklet series serves the purpose of uncovering national problems before the crisis, government coping strategies, stimulus plans, potential prospects, and challenges of each individual country, and the interdependence between countries. The 6 years of data allow us to compare NIC and economic development crossing before, during, and after the financial crisis. They are handy booklets for readers to have a quick yet overall view of countries of personal interest. The list of 48 countries in 11 clusters is provided in the appendix of each booklet.

Searching for financial crisis-related literature for 48 countries is itself a very daunting task, not to mention summarizing and analyzing it. For financial crisis-related literature, we mainly relied on the reports and statistics of certain world organizations, including OECD, World Bank, United Nations, International Monetary Fund (IMF), European Commission Office, the US Congressional Research Service, the U.S. Central Intelligence Agency, and International Labor Office (ILO). Some reliable research centers, such as the National Bureau of

Economic Research in the U.S., World Economic Forum, the Heritage Foundation in the U.S., and government websites from each country were also our sources of information. Due to the requirement of more update and comprehensive information, we were not able to use as much academic literature as we would have liked, because it generally covers a very specific topic with time lag and with research methods not easily comprehended by the general public. Therefore, we had to resort to some online news reports for more current information.

In the middle of 2012, the lasting financial troubles caused the European economy to tilt back into a recession, which also slowed down economic growth across the globe. However, almost 4 years have passed since the outbreak of the global financial crisis in late 2008; it is about time to reflect on what happened and the impact of the financial crisis. By comparing so many countries, we came to a preliminary conclusion that countries with faster recovery from the financial crisis have higher NIC than those with slower recovery. In other words, countries that rebounded fast from the crisis generally have solid NIC fundamentals, including human capital, market capital, process capital, and renewal capital. We also found that the higher the NIC, the higher the GDP per capita (ppp). This booklet series provides a different perspective to look beyond the traditional economic indicators for national development.

In an era when IA have become a key competitive advantage, investing in NIC development is investing in future national development and well-being.

Enjoy!

Carol Yeh-Yun Lin
Professor, Department of Business Adminstration
National Chengchi University, Taiwan
Taiwan Intellectual Capital Research Center (TICRC)

Executive Summary

> *Retention of the talent is a challenging task that requires more national intellectual capital support.*

How can national intellectual capital (NIC) be supportive as a policy guideline for national well-being? A key factor in the financial crisis was the conventional financial system failed to detect potential risks due to non-transparent information disclosure. Our earlier NIC research has revealed certain warning signs of impending financial crisis for Greece, Iceland, and Ireland. Such findings indicate that NIC, albeit intangible, can provide valuable insights into future risk control and strategy formulation. This booklet looks into the connections between the 2008 global financial crisis and NIC development.

Based on data covering 2005–2010 for 48 countries, the figures and tables presented in this volume largely reflect situations in the real economy, with some statistics showing early warnings before the financial crisis. Data of 48 countries indicate that the higher the NIC, the higher the GDP per capita (ppp), accentuating the value of NIC in major countries throughout the world. *For the six-year average NIC ranking, Israel ranked 6th, Jordan 33rd, South Africa 37th, and Turkey 36th.*

The 2008 financial crisis is considered to be the worst since the Great Depression of the 1930s, with severe impacts all across the globe. This financial crisis came with unexpected speed and spread into a global economic shock, which resulted in a number of European bank failures. During this period, economies worldwide slowed, credits tightened, and international trade declined. Governments and central banks worldwide responded to the crisis with unprecedented fiscal stimuli, monetary policy expansions, and institutional bailouts in their respective countries. While the financial crisis was officially declared over by the end of 2009, as of late 2012 Europe was tilted back to a recession. For the first three quarters in 2012, the U.S. reported only modest growth, even the champion recovery region, Asia, was also experiencing economic slowdowns due to the gloomy external environment.

At the initial stage of this global financial crisis, the reported four countries fared relatively well. Yet when global credits tightened and export demands drastically dropped, their economies failed to withstand the impact, as nowadays any problem in the West will have a global impact via trade and financial linkages.

Signs of recovery of these countries began to show in late 2009 and early 2010. However, with global economy slowed at the second half of 2010, recovery of these four countries also slowed; started from 2011 and extended to 2012.

As of mid-2012, Israel's economy weathered through this financial crisis in relatively good shape but still suffers alongside others from the continuing effects of the renewed global crisis with its increased geopolitical tensions. Jordan's economic outlook entails both opportunities and challenges. Its increasing economic openness, highly capitalized and regulated banking sector are positives. However, its high unemployment, high social pressures, persistent fiscal and current account deficits, and the volatile regional political environment cloud its future development prospects. The pace of South Africa's recovery has slowed as a result of weak external demand, negative effects of the global slowdown on consumer and investor confidence, and its domestic labor unrest. In Turkey, economic activity decelerated in the second half of 2011 with the weakening of external demand and policy measures to curb domestic demand. However, growth was projected to recover gradually in 2012 as confidence and international conditions improved.

In general, the NIC of these four countries resides in the third quartile among 48 countries. The exception is Israel, which ranked number six. Human capital and renewal capital, two long-term NIC values, for the four countries did not fluctuate much before and after the financial crisis. However, the two short-term NIC, market capital and process capital, started to decline from 2006 in South Africa, from 2007 in both Israel and Jordan, and from 2008 in Turkey. South Africa had the fastest short-term NIC rebound from 2008, followed by Israel in 2009, and Jordan and Turkey in 2010. In terms of NIC ranking changes over three time periods (2005–2006, 2007–2008, and 2009–2010), Jordan had the greatest NIC ranking declines, indicating that it lost international competitiveness in NIC after the financial crisis. On the contrary, South Africa and Turkey had relatively large-scale NIC ranking gains.

The 3D trajectory analysis reveals that *human capital and government-related issues are the two greatest barricades* to achieve GDP growth in this country cluster. Issues of concern include public expenditure on education, higher education enrollment, employee training, capital availability, transparency of government policy, and corporate tax encouragement. The areas that need further enhancements are quite similar for these four countries, including more emphasis on building renewal capital (patents—4 counts, business R&D—3 counts, and basic research—2 counts) and providing better infrastructure (computers in use per capita—4 counts and internet subscribers—2 counts) in the knowledge economy.

This economic crisis provides an ideal opportunity for nations to examine the soundness of their economic system and the effectiveness of national governance related to NIC. The following implications are drawn from our research findings. Readers can refer to Chap 5 for the rationale behind these implications.

1. National intellectual capital development goes together with the economic development and should be regarded as an enhancer of economic growth.

2. Establishing a more effective national and NIC governance system to monitor national adherence to international financial standard is essential.
3. National growth strategy needs to be revisited and refined for sustainable national and NIC development.
4. Dependence on capital inflows needs to be gradually balanced by domestic financial support and NIC support.
5. Government needs to aggressively launch structural reforms for a more business-friendly and value creating internal as well as external environment.
6. Export diversification can be pursued to spread financial risk with NIC support.
7. Social partnership facilitates an economy to weather through the financial crisis and becomes valuable national process capital.
8. Capitalizing national NIC strength is a sustainable way for future economic development and well-being.
9. Retention of the talents is a challenging task that requires more NIC support.

In general, countries reported in this volume recovered relatively well after the 2008 global financial crisis. International financial rating agencies also showed confidence in the future prospects of these countries. However, for sustainable national development, common areas that need special attention include geopolitical tension, relatively high unemployment rate, poverty, inequality, workforce productivity, and increasing government debt and deficit. The aftermath of the financial crisis provides the best opportunity for these countries to review their national growth strategies and to continue structural reforms.

In an era when intangible assets have become key competitive advantages, investing in national intellectual capital development is equivalent to investing in future economic development and well-being. National intellectual capital evolution can be nourished both from a local culture viewpoint as well as from a global interconnectivity via social media perspective.

Based on emerging new insights into values, societal history and citizen relationships, a key focus for the future will be the fusion of national intellectual capital, social service innovation, and societal innovation to enable a new societal fabric.

Contents

List of Figures

List of Tables

Appendices

Abstract

In the first decade of the new millennium, the biggest event that caught worldwide attention was the 2008 global financial crisis, which was brought about primarily by ineffective governance, failed surveillance systems, and implementation flaws. These problems are mainly intangible in nature. Therefore, examining the financial crisis from the viewpoint of intangible asset provides a different perspective from traditional economic approaches.

National intellectual capital (NIC), mainly consisting of human capital, market capital, process capital, renewal capital, and financial capital, is a valuable intangible asset and a key source of national competitive advantage in today's knowledge economy. This booklet looks into the connections between the 2008 global financial crisis and NIC development with a special focus on Israel, Jordan, South Africa, and Turkey.

In addition to the summaries of financial crisis impact, the aftermath, future prospects, and challenges of each individual country, NIC analysis based on data covering 2005–2010 for 48 countries reveal that the higher the NIC, the higher the GDP per capita (ppp). Graphical presentations of various types allow for intra-country and inter-country comparisons to position the reported four countries on a world map of NIC–GDP co-development.

By looking into tangible economic development along with intangible NIC development, this booklet provides valuable implications for policymakers.

Keywords Competitiveness · Economic policy · Financial capital · Human capital · Innovation · Intangible assets · Intellectual capital · Knowledge management · Research and development (R&D) · Science and technology policy

Chapter 1
Introduction

The 2008 global financial crisis is considered by many economists to be the worst one since the Great Depression of the 1930s. The crisis rapidly developed and spread into a global economic shock, which resulted in a number of European bank failures (Altman 2009; Fackler 2009). World political leaders, national ministers of finance, and central bank directors coordinated their efforts to reduce fear, but the crisis continued and eventually led to a global currency crisis. During this period, economies worldwide slowed, credits tightened, and international trade declined.

After the full force of the financial crisis hit in October 2008, there was a call in the United States for a hands-off policy in order to let the markets "work themselves out," in accordance with how capitalism was theoretically supposed to work. Yet, U.S. Federal Reserve Chairman Ben Bernanke believed that such a policy would be catastrophic and urged government intervention. In a statement to Congress, Mr. Bernanke said that, "If we let the banking system fail, no one will talk about the Great Depression anymore, because this will be so much worse" (Reavis 2009). As a result of this, the U.S. government decided to take action to prevent such a failure.

Following the lead of the United States, governments and central banks worldwide responded to the international crisis with unprecedented fiscal stimuli, monetary policy expansions, and institutional bailouts in their respective countries. The financial rescue worked and an economic crisis akin to the Great Depression was avoided. It was subsequently declared over at the end of 2009 (Kehoe 2010). After a short global recovery in 2010, the economy slowed again mainly due to continued financial troubles in the Euro area starting the second half of 2011.

During the early stages of the financial crisis, management scholars criticized traditional accounting system's inability to reveal the intangibles that explain hidden risks as well as values for proper decision making (Reavis 2009). In line with highlighting the importance of the intangibles, intellectual capital (Edvinsson and Malone 1997) advocates the value inherent in measures such as human capital and social capital, which has gained increasing attention in today's keener global competition.

C. Y.-Y. Lin et al., *National Intellectual Capital and the Financial Crisis in Israel, Jordan, South Africa, and Turkey*, SpringerBriefs in Economics,
DOI: 10.1007/978-1-4614-7981-9_1,

It is our deep belief that national intellectual capital (NIC), albeit intangible, can provide valuable insights to policy makers regarding future risk control and strategy formulation. Our previous book, *National Intellectual Capital: A Comparison of 40 Countries* (Lin and Edvinsson 2011; www.nic40.org), was born out of this belief and traces the NIC development of 40 countries over a 14-year period from 1995 to 2008. The data analysis presented in our previous work revealed certain warning signs of impending financial crisis for countries such as Greece, Iceland, and Ireland (Lin and Edvinsson 2011: 327–333). As a follow-up study, this booklet series is an attempt to further understand the connections between the financial crisis and NIC development.

The booklet series, in its entirety, will examine the NIC statuses of 48 countries from the period of 2005–2010 to glean new understanding about whether there is a NIC development pattern that distinguishes the fast-recovery from the slow-recovery countries. This is presented through a series of 11 country clusters, with each booklet focusing on one particular cluster. The clusters are selected based on several factors: geographical proximity, geographical size, or the country's phase of economic development. Focusing on one cluster at a time, we first probe the issues of concern within a single country, then extend to compare the cluster as a whole to see whether the situation before and after the crisis can be explained by the intangible NIC. Our data come from the well-recognized International institute for management development (IMD) in Switzerland. The IMD has been publishing yearly rankings of World Competitiveness for around two decades. It is hoped that the analysis in this booklet series can provide a different perspective of the financial crisis for future policy implications.

This volume, the fifth in this series, will focus on Israel, Jordan, South Africa, and Turkey as they have either geographical proximity or similar levels of economic development. This booklet will first provide an economic background to these four countries as a whole before going into each individual country's development. Through this process, the authors hope to paint a general picture of the economic condition and provide a basis for our dataset and analysis in future sections. Next, Chap. 2 will briefly introduce the impact of the 2008 financial crisis on the four countries. Chapter 3 elaborates the NIC development of these four countries. Chapter 4 describes issues beyond the financial crisis and Chap. 5 concludes with future perspective and policy implications.

Economic Background

Since the economic history of these four countries goes back centuries, it is impossible to cover the entire spectrum in our work. As such, this background discussion will consider events in the relative recent history from 2005 onwards that have the most direct impact upon the current economic conditions of each specific country. In addition, particular attention will be given to the 2008 global financial crisis. In doing so, the authors hope that the background, in conjunction with our later data and analysis, will provide a "before, during, and after" picture of what was happening from a macroeconomic and intangible assets viewpoint.

In the middle of 2012, the world economy slowed down again, due to the continued financial troubles in some Euro countries and modest recovery in the U.S. However, in 2011, all four countries reported in this volume had recovered from the 2008 global financial crisis, albeit to varying degrees. To paint a general picture about their global competitiveness in the most recent years and before the financial crisis, we introduce hereunder the Global Competitiveness Index (GCI) published by the World Economic Forum for readers' reference. This index is relatively robust, for it takes into account the 12 distinct pillars[1] containing basic requirements, efficiency enhancers, and innovation factors that contribute to a nation's overall economic strength. Based upon commonly accepted economic theory, the development of 142 countries was split into three stages, in which different factors play a dominant role in determining the outcome of a country's economy. Stage 1, Stage 2, and Stage 3 are, respectively, characterized by being factor, efficiency, and innovation driven (Schwab 2011). In the 2011–2012 GCI report, Israel was categorized as Stage 3, Jordan and South Africa Stage 2, and Turkey Stage 2.5.

Taking each country's annual ranking and plotting against a time series of seven periods, Fig. 1.1 displays a rough pictorial overview of the four countries' global competitiveness changes before and after the financial crisis.

From Fig. 1.1, it can be seen that over the past 7 years, the GCI ranking of Israel has advanced from number 27 to number 22; Jordan declined from number 45 to number 71, South Africa declined from number 42 to number 50, and Turkey advanced from number 66 to number 59. Jordan's GCI decline coincides with its fallen economy after the financial crisis.

Right after the financial crisis, the world economy rebounded well in 2010, by around 4.3 % with a sizeable, synchronized, and successful policy stimulus (Lyons 2011). In addition, the recovery strength of emerging economies also helped the global growth. However, it was slowed at the second half of 2010, mainly because Europe fell into another recession. Emerging economies were again not decoupled but better insulated, as any problems in the West will have a global impact via trade and financial linkages. As a result, recovery of these four countries also slowed starting from 2011 and extending into 2012.

As of mid-2012, Israel's economy recovered from this financial crisis in relatively good shape but still suffers alongside others from the continuing effects of the renewed global crisis with its increased geopolitical tensions. Jordan's economic outlook entails both opportunities and challenges. Its increasing economic openness, highly capitalized and regulated banking sector, and continuous external donor support are positive. However, its high unemployment, high social

---

[1] The 12 pillars include: institutions, infrastructure, macroeconomic environment, health and primary education, higher education and training, goods market efficiency, labor market efficiency, financial market development, technological readiness, market size, business sophistication, and innovation.

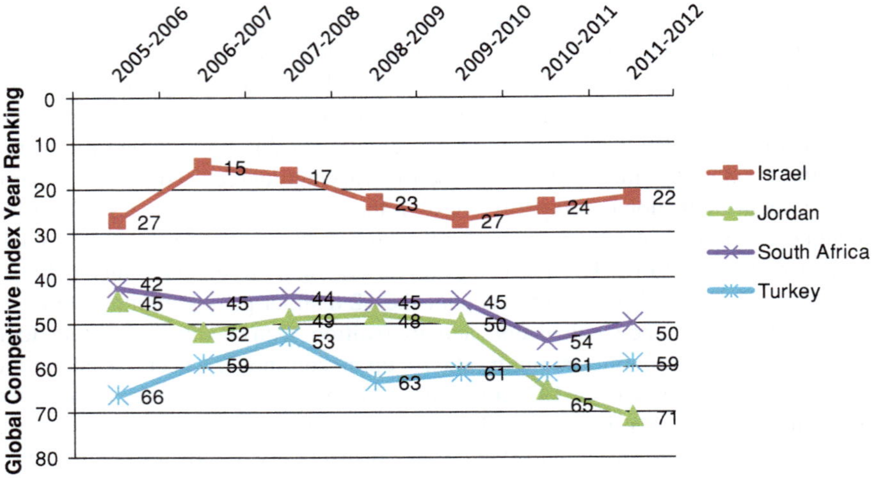

Fig. 1.1 GCI ranking of Israel, Jordan, South Africa, and Turkey

pressures, persistent fiscal and current account deficits, and the volatile regional political environment cloud its future development (Barakat et al. 2012). The pace of South Africa's recovery has slowed as a result of weak external demand, negative effects of the global slowdown on consumer and investor confidence, and its domestic labor unrest. In Turkey, economic activity decelerated markedly in the second half of 2011 with weakening of external demand and policy measures to curb domestic demand. However, growth is projected to recover gradually in 2012 as confidence and international conditions improve, reaching 3.25 % in 2012 and 4.5 % in 2013 (OECD 2012). The next chapter will give a brief background and qualitative analysis of the 2008 global financial crisis as it relates to these four countries.

Chapter 2
Impact of 2008 Global Financial Crisis

The 2008 financial crisis rapidly developed and spread into a global economic shock. Economies worldwide slowed during this period due to tightening credit and drops in international trade. At the onset of the financial crisis, policy makers of all four countries thought that they could be decoupled from the crisis, as their banks kept a conservative model and did not invest deeply in high-risk securities or complex instruments. However, that view quickly changed following the rapid global trade decline, thus eroding the prospects for exports. As liquidity issues became more challenging, investors began to withdraw funds from emerging markets in a capital flight as a risk aversion measure (Baxter 2012). Furthermore, consumers in the major markets such as European Union and the U.S. cut their spending to save their personal wealth, thus decreased the trade demand and impacted those export-reliant countries.

A major reason for this global financial shock resulted from the neoliberalization of the world economy over the last 30 years, along with the rise of uncontrolled financial flows, the increasingly uneven geographical development, and economic technocracy (Balaban 2009). Based on Standard & Poor's (S&P) 2008 estimation, around US$25 trillion in asset values was wiped out at the global level, due to the unwinding of the leverage created by the global sub-prime financial crisis (Baxter 2012).

For the entire world, around US$2 trillion in stimulus packages, amounting to approximately 3 % of world Gross Domestic Product, has been invested, exceeding the call by the international monetary fund (IMF) for 2 % of global GDP to counter the financial crisis (Nanto 2009). As of mid-2012, several European countries were still suffering from the sovereign debt problem, such as the second bailout for Greece in March 2012 and financial assistance for Spain in June 2012.

In order to give a general idea of how the 2008 global financial crisis impacted these four countries, we first compare their real GDP growth, total general government debt, unemployment rate, and consumer price inflation (CPI). Then, we briefly describe the conditions of Israel, Jordan, South Africa, and Turkey in sequence.

C. Y.-Y. Lin et al., *National Intellectual Capital and the Financial Crisis in Israel, Jordan, South Africa, and Turkey*, SpringerBriefs in Economics,
DOI: 10.1007/978-1-4614-7981-9_2, © The Author(s) 2014

Comparisons of the Four Countries

Figure 2.1 shows that all four countries had an obvious GDP growth decline starting in 2008 and reaching its lowest level in 2009. In 2010, none of the country has recovered its GDP growth to the pre-crisis level. Among the four countries, Jordan has the least amount of fluctuation over the 6 years. Turkey had the widest range of fluctuation, from its highest growth rate of 7.03 % in 2005, to its lowest rate of −5.93 % in 2009, then to a high growth of 4.24 % in 2010. In addition, Turkey experienced an earlier growth decline in 2008 and bounced back in 2010, faster than the other three countries.

Figure 2.2 indicates the development of total general government debt percentage GDP of the four countries from 2005 to 2010. All four countries had relatively stable government debt over the years, except Jordan had a larger scale of debt reduction. Different from other country clusters, these four countries reduced their government debt after the financial crisis to lower than their 2005 debt level. In 2010, their government debt only increased mildly, comparing to either 2008 or 2009 debt level. All through the years, Israel has the highest debt level, followed by Jordan, Turkey, and South Africa. In 2010, Israel's government debt still exceeds the 60 % limit suggested by the EU.

Reinhart and Rogoff (2009) reported findings from their research on financial crises over the last 800 years that the aftermath of a financial crisis brings slow and halted growth, sustained high unemployment, and surging public debt—with the overhang of public and private debt being the most important impediment to a normal recovery from the recession.

Figure 2.3 shows the unemployment rate of this country cluster from 2005 to 2010. Interestingly, all four countries had unemployment rate reductions in 2008

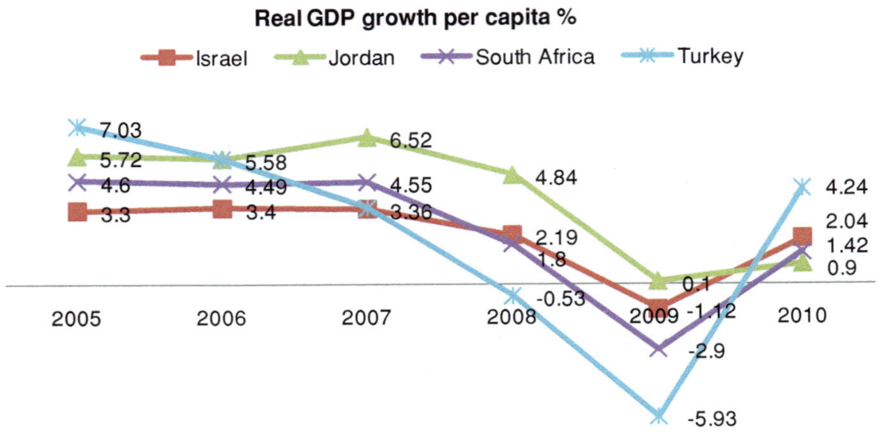

Fig. 2.1 Real GDP growth per capita of Israel, Jordan, South Africa, and Turkey from 2005 to 2010

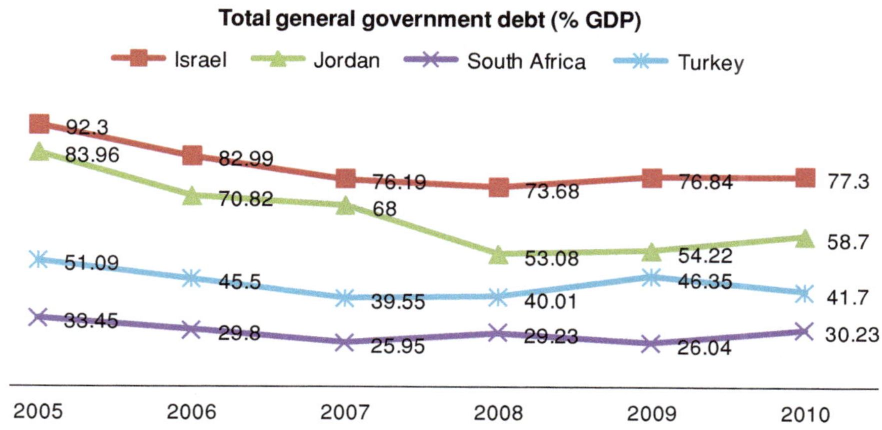

Fig. 2.2 Total general government debt (% GDP) of Israel, Jordan, South Africa, and Turkey from 2005 to 2010

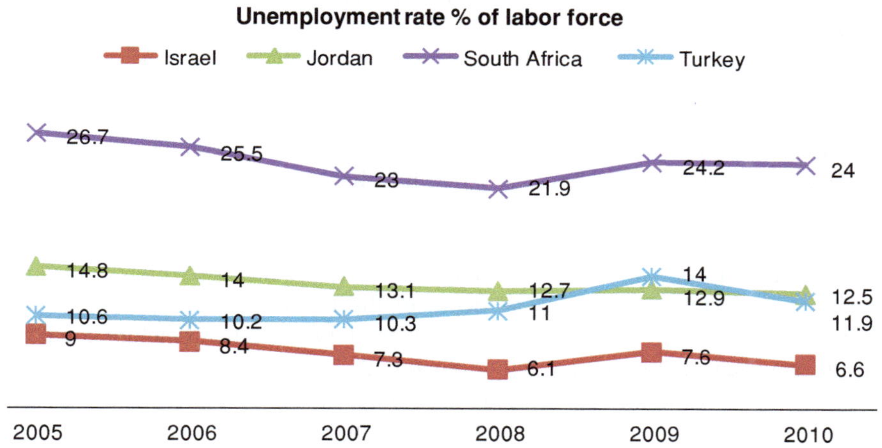

Fig. 2.3 Unemployment rate of Israel, Jordan, South Africa, and Turkey from 2005 to 2010

(except Turkey), then a slight increase in 2009, indicating the financial crisis did not seriously impact them until 2009. Overall, the ratios are relatively stable. In 2010, with the exception of Turkey, unemployment rate was even lower than that of 2005. Among the four countries, South Africa had the highest unemployment ratio all through the years, which was almost three times that of Israel and twice that of Jordan and Turkey.

Figure 2.4 shows the CPI of the four countries from 2005 to 2010. All four countries had a CPI hike in 2008, and then a reduction in 2009, with Jordan having the most drastic CPI fluctuation during the financial crisis, from 13.94 % in 2008

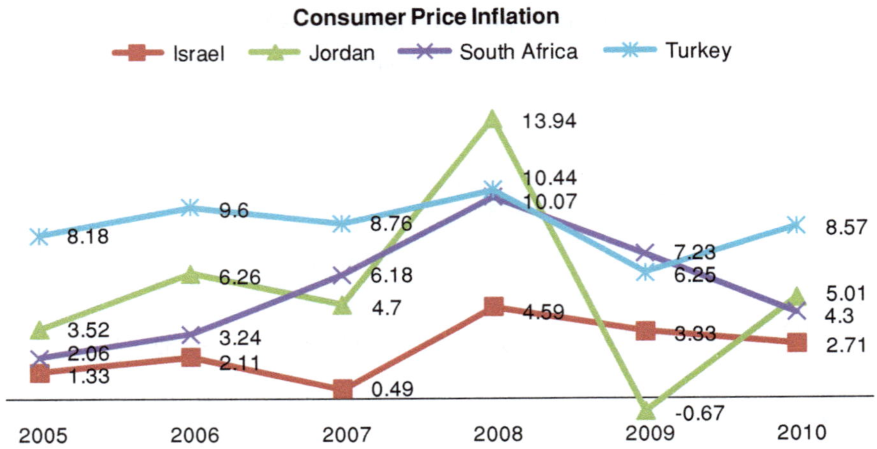

Fig. 2.4 Consumer price inflation of Israel, Jordan, South Africa, and Turkey from 2005 to 2010

plummeted to −0.67 % in 2009. In 2010, all the countries had higher CPI than their 2005 statuses.

In general, the four figures for these four countries indicate that real GDP growth per capita and CPI were clearly impacted by the 2008 global financial crisis. The total general government debt and unemployment rate do not vary much before and after the financial crisis, except in Jordan with government debt and in Turkey with the unemployment rate. In general, Israel has the most serious government debt problem, Jordan is most unstable in CPI, South Africa's unemployment rate is the highest, and Turkey has the highest fluctuation in GDP growth.

In what follows, we briefly describe the impact of the 2008 global financial crisis on these four countries. The depth of the report depends on the English literature available for each country. For readers to gain a general picture about the efforts that each country has put into mitigating the negative impact of the financial crisis, we have summarized the details of stimulus packages implemented by these countries in Appendix 1. Please note that the reported package is based on publicly available data and is not an exhaustive list. In addition, the reported amounts of stimulus packages were based on the foreign exchange rate at the time of each stimulus, and thus vary. Readers can also refer to Appendix 2 for the important meetings conducted by key global leaders during this financial crisis.

Israel

Israel has a technologically advanced market economy. Its GDP, after contracting slightly in 2001 and 2002 due to the Palestinian conflict and troubles in the high-technology sector (dot.com bubbles), grew about 5 % per year from 2004 to 2007

(CIA 2012). The 2008 global financial crisis spurred only a brief recession in Israel (CIA 2012; Rosenberg 2010). The country entered the crisis with solid fundamentals with a resilient banking sector, years of prudent fiscal policy, a series of liberalizing reforms, high growth rate, low unemployment rate, and current account surplus (Buchwald 2009; CIA 2012; Friedberg 2009). The global economic downturn affected Israel's economy primarily through reduced demand for its exports in the United States and EU (total 70 % of Israeli exports), as exports of goods and services accounted for about 40 % of the country's GDP (Buchwald 2009; CIA 2012). Although Israel was not immune from the global economic crisis, its economy fared better than other developed economies with a relatively early recovery (Buchwald 2009; CIA 2012; Friedberg 2009). According to an OECD survey, the Israeli economy was the last among 29 economies to enter into a recession (fourth quarter 2008) and among the first to exit (second quarter 2009), making it by far the shortest downturn among the group (Rosenberg 2010).

Still maintaining a positive GDP growth in 2008, Israel slipped to negative GDP growth in 2009 (Fig. 2.1). However, foreign direct investment (FDI) in Israel did not suffer from this economic downturn. In 2008, its FDI totaled US$10.5 billion, up US$500 million from 2007 and its high-tech companies have been able to raise US$2.08 billion from local and foreign venture investors, 18 % above the US$1.76 billion raised in 2007 (Buchwald 2009).

The Israeli Government responded to the recession by implementing a modest fiscal stimulus package and an aggressive expansionary monetary policy—including cutting interest rates to record lows, purchasing government bonds, and intervening in the foreign currency market (CIA 2012; Rosenberg 2010). At the end of 2008, the Bank of Israel dropped down the basic interest rate gradually from a level of 4.25 % in September 2008 to the historic low of 0.5 % in April 2009 (Brosh 2011). Furthermore, the Bank of Israel also purchased government bonds for a limited period of time to reduce the financing costs for the business sector. It also intervened in the foreign currency market, by purchasing billions of dollars in supporting the exchange rate of the shekel (Israeli currency) and the profitability of exports (Brosh 2011). As of January 2009 the central bank had bought a total of, approximately, US$10 billion, increasing the foreign exchange reserves to about $37 billion (State of Israel 2012).

To help safeguard the economy, Israel's Ministry of Finance and central bank also implemented special initiatives including an acceleration program, a pension safety net and a monetary program to help increase liquidity, create new jobs, protect private savings, and promote continuous growth in Israel (State of Israel 2012). The acceleration program allocates funds to infrastructure, research and development, the credit sector, and the labor market with an emphasis on small and medium-size businesses that have fewer resources available to deal with the credit crunch. All the above-stated activities were expected to increase the supply of credit by around US$625 million (2.5 billion shekels) (State of Israel 2012). In addition, the government offered as much as US$3 billion (12 billion shekels) in guarantees to commercial banks to help them raise capital, but the banks in the end had no need of the assistance (Rosenberg 2010). The Israeli government also supported a bailout of the affected pension funds and provided certain guarantees to workers age 57 and above (Buchwald 2009). Other than the government, Mizrahi Tefahot Bank, the Manufacturers Association of Israel, and the Mutual Fund of Employers launched a joint initiative to help mid-sized businesses (20–100 employees) cope with the economic crisis. The parties signed an agreement to set up a loan fund of up to US$200 million (Buchwald 2009).

Throughout the crisis, manufacturers implemented flexible methods of employment, such as reducing overtime, collective vacations, and shortening of working week, which enabled them to avoid widespread dismissals and retain skilled workers for "the day after" (Brosh 2011). Another significant factor, which contributed to the resilience of Israeli industry during the 2008 crisis, was the coincidence that at the end of 2008 and the beginning of 2009, Intel's new plant commenced operations in Israel. By the end of 2009, the plant reached exports of more than US$3 billion, contributing about 6 % of Israeli industrial export growth (Brosh 2011).

During the financial crisis, leading international rating agencies continue to express confidence in the Israeli economy. Fitch maintained its foreign currency issuer default rating (IDR) for Israel at "A" with a stable outlook, and its local currency IDR at a stable A+. International rating company S&P and Moody's also kept their original ratings, with S&P stating "the rating affirmation reflects the government's commitment to continued fiscal discipline and the resilience of the Israeli economy" (State of Israel 2012). As a result, in March 2009, Israel launched a benchmark 10-year U.S. dollar denominated global bond issue worth US$1.5 billion. Demands for this issue exceeded US$12 billion, and were purchased by over 300 investors in 14 different countries (Buchwald 2009). It is a sign that investors continue to view Israel as an attractive investment in times of high global economy turmoil.

Recovery began in Israel's industrial exports, immediately with the recovery in world trade, and was very rapid. Since the third quarter of 2009, industrial exports recorded quarterly growth of about 9 % on average, amounting to a real aggregate growth of 29 % within three quarters (Brosh 2011).

Jordan

Jordan has a market-oriented economy with abundant skilled human resources (Jaradat 2010). However, its economy is among the smallest in the Middle East, with insufficient supplies of water, oil, and other natural resources, underlying the government's heavy reliance on foreign assistance (CIA 2012). The economy is supported to a significant degree by foreign loans, international aid, and remittances from expatriate workers (Heritage 2012). Its service-oriented economy constitutes about 64 % of its GDP (Jaradat 2010). Since 1989, Jordan has successfully implemented several economic adjustment programs, in collaboration with the IMF and the World Bank, and support from the International Community (Jaradat 2010).

Jordan, like other countries around the world, was affected by the global financial crisis, but to a lesser extent due to the lack of modern financial instruments such as derivatives (Alnajjar et al. 2011; Ammon News 2009). As a country that relies primarily on imports, Jordan initially benefited from the decrease in prices of oil and other commodities (Ammon News 2009). In addition, the majority of banks were well capitalized (Al-Mahrouq 2009) and Jordan's limited integration with global financial markets buffered it from the 2008 global financial turmoil, preventing major losses among banks or capital flight (Larbi 2009; Mansur 2011).

In 2008, despite certain macroeconomic complications (high inflation rate, current account deficit, budget deficit, etc.), Jordan maintained positive developments. Although, its real GDP growth in 2008 slid (Fig. 2.1), its FDIs increased. When economies in the developed world fell, investors were seeking a safe haven for their funds and found Jordan was safe (Mansur 2011). At the beginning of global financial crisis, Jordan still managed to attract more tourists. The number of visitors to the country reached 7.1 million in 2008, compared to 6.5 million in 2007 (an increase of 8.8 %) (Al-Mahrouq 2009).

However, the global economic slowdown depressed Jordan's GDP growth (CIA 2012) with delayed effect. The economy, after a positive GDP growth in 2008, witnessed a setback in 2009 showing almost zero growth (Fig. 2.1). In addition, industrial production decreased, producer prices decreased, and share prices which had started to decline during the last quarter of 2008 continued to decline in 2009 (Mansur 2011). Export-oriented sectors such as manufacturing, mining, and the transport of re-exports was hit the hardest. The kingdom's overall exports and re-exports dropped by 15.6 % during the first seven months of 2009, compared the same period a year before (Ammon News 2009).

The Central Bank of Jordan has taken preemptive steps to maintain confidence and support the domestic money market by tightening regulations in the banking sector, and cutting key interest rates twice (Al-Mahrouq 2009; Larbi 2009). In addition, the government fully guaranteed all bank deposits in local and foreign currencies as well as inter-bank lending until the end of 2009 (Al-Mahrouq 2009). To overcome major imbalances and to regain macroeconomic stability for sustainable economic growth, home grown reform programs were being implemented including the National Agenda Initiative—a sizeable government contribution where general government expenditures reached 44.6 % of GDP in 2008 (Jaradat 2010). Its medium term fiscal policy measures include public sector employment freeze, limit salaries increase, restructuring and merging similar government institutions, controlling the government's consumption of petroleum products, gradually reducing the grants provided from the central government to other government entities, lowering the current expenditure component of capital expenditures, prioritizing capital expenditures, improving the efficiency of revenues collection and limiting tax evasion, and issuing new law and amending relevant laws to mobilize domestic investment and attract FDIs (Jaradat 2010).

The Jordanian economy did not do well after the crisis, in spite of early predictions that it was sheltered from its impact and later on the Central Bank of Jordan has empowered domestic banks to avoid the risks as encountered by international banking institutions (Al-Mahrouq 2009). Critics complained that "the government's handling of the crisis was reactionary, not precautionary" and being very conservative and focused on borrowing from abroad (Ammon News 2009).

South Africa

South Africa is a middle-income, emerging market with an abundant supply of natural resources. It has well-developed financial, legal, communications, and transport sectors with modern infrastructure supporting a relatively efficient distribution of goods to major urban centers throughout the region (CIA 2012). Since its turn toward democracy in 1994, South Africa has improved its reputation as the leading economic power in Africa and has increasingly attracted global investors (Draper et al. 2009). Continuing integration into global commerce has led to notable increases in its productivity (Heritage 2012). Growth was robust from 2004 to 2007 as South Africa reaped the benefits of macroeconomic stability and a global commodities boom (CIA 2012; OECD 2010).

However, South Africa's economy began to slow in the second half of 2007 due to the electricity crisis (CIA 2012). The global downturn struck South Africa when it had already passed the boom, and the economy slowed sharply, experiencing its first recession in 17 years (OECD 2010). Thus, it entered the crisis with a greater degree of vulnerability, having a large current account deficit, high interest rates, and high inflation (Padayachee n.d.). The high interest rate has halted growth in private consumption (OECD 2010).

South Africa's decline was led by manufacturing and mining where the sudden drop in export demand was reflected in a sharp reduction in private investment and subsequently in falling employment. Its GDP figures for the last quarter of 2008 came in negative, with manufacturing falling by 21.8 %, the automobile industry declining over 30 % year-on-year, and mining production reducing greatly as global commodity prices remain depressed (Zini 2009). Afterward, job creation slowed down, consumers' expenditure declined, credit extension to the private sector slowed, and housing prices dropped (Zini 2009). Unemployment was already high prior to the crisis and began rising further from the fourth quarter of 2008 (ILO 2010). Consequently, the country experienced a sharp deceleration of growth from more than 5 % in 2007 to a fall of almost 2 % in 2009 (OECD 2010). The *Johannesburg Securities Exchange* all-share index fell from a high of 32,542 on May 23, 2008 to a low of 18,066 on November 21, 2008 (Padayachee n.d.). From October 2008, it suffered from capital withdrawal and a depreciation of its currency, the Rand (Draper et al. 2009). In December 2008 tripartite negotiations began among organized labor, business and government to formulate a collective response to the crisis (ILO 2010)

However, South Africa's decline in output was moderated by a countercyclical policy response, made possible by past fiscal prudence and by the resilience of the non-impacted banking system (OECD 2010). Furthermore, to remedy the problems, the government's policy response prompted a focus on housing, education, social protection, public works, and health programs under the expansionary budget (Zini 2009). In addition, the Training Layoff Scheme, rolled out in September 2009, provides skills training and an allowance to employees during a negotiated layoff period, although they technically remain employed (ILO 2010).

Nevertheless, South Africa's downturn was fairly shallow: the peak-to-trough fall in output was smaller than in most OECD countries and emerging market economies (OECD 2010). There were several reasons for this mild impact including: absence of bank failures; strong profitability in the banking sector; low levels of nonperforming loans and comfortable capital cushions; banks' lack of direct exposure to problem assets from the U.S. and Europe; bankruptcy laws that favor creditors in recovering collateral for bad loans; and conservative approaches on the part of both the regulator and the bank themselves (OECD 2010). With healthy foreign reserves and continuous financial inflows, South Africa had no problem funding the deficit of around −3.9 % in 2009/2010 (Zini 2009). Therefore, despite South Africa's economy having been hard hit by the global financial crisis, no exchange rate shock or "sudden stop" was experienced (Draper et al. 2009).

Another important factor that mitigated the impact of the crisis impact was the fact that the previously approved ambitious capital expenditure plans in energy and transport by public enterprises were not revised downwards, which greatly supported output during the decline. Monetary policy was also eased, but not particularly aggressively. No emergency actions, such as capital support for banks or quantitative easing to support lower interest rates, were needed (OECD 2010).

Turkey

Turkey's economy has been increasingly driven by its industry and service sectors. An aggressive privatization program has reduced state involvement in basic industry, banking, transport, and communication, and an emerging cadre of middle-class entrepreneurs is adding dynamism to the economy (CIA 2012). After Turkey experienced a severe financial crisis in 2001, Ankara adopted financial and fiscal reforms as part of an IMF program. The reforms strengthened the country's economic fundamentals and Turkey experienced a strong and sustained period of economic expansion after the 2001 recession, with gross domestic product (GDP) growing at an average annual rate of 6.8 % between 2002 and 2007 (CIA 2012; ILO 2010b; Rawdanowicz 2010).

The global financial crisis hit Turkey in September 2008. Actually, the resilience of Turkish domestic banks improved after its 1994 and 2001 debt crises (Rodrik 2009). However Turkey's problematic growth strategy, which heavily relied on the foreign capital inflows, was predicted to eventually end up with a domestic economic crisis (Balaban 2009). Its decline in GDP growth rate started even before the 2008 global financial crisis hit the Turkish economy (Balaban 2009); that is, in 2006 as exhibited in Fig. 2.1. As a result, Turkey was hit worse in many ways by this financial crisis than in its previous 1994 and 2001 crises. According to IMF , Turkey is one of the few countries that were adversely affected by the crisis to such a large extent (Togan 2010). Exports declined by 13 % in the last quarter of 2008 and 30 % in the January–July period of 2009 (Babacan 2009).

Despite Turkey's general economic slowdown, the soundness of its banking sector provided a buffer against external shocks and the absence of toxic assets also prevented the sector from experiencing write-downs and government bailouts (Babacan 2009; Heritage 2012; Rawdanowicz 2010). Although the banking and financial sector remained relatively robust during the crisis, the real economy was significantly affected, mostly through the international trade channel (Yorukoglu and Atasoy 2012). The sharp contraction in global economic activity, weak domestic demand conditions, sudden stops in external capital flows, negative confidence effects, and structural problems did affect the Turkish economy adversely (Rawdanowicz 2010; Togan 2010). During 2009, GDP was expected to decline by 6 % according to the government and by 6.5 % according to the IMF . IMD database showed −5.93 % GDP growth in 2009 (Fig. 2.2). The decrease stemmed mainly from declines in private investment and private consumption expenditures, stocks, and exports of goods and services (Togan 2010).

With the slowing down of Turkey's real economy, unemployment rose. The number of people receiving unemployment insurance more than doubled from 221,600 in 2007 to 471,600 in 2009 (ILO 2010b). Nearly 2.7 million unemployed individuals were in the urban sector, where the unemployment rate was 16 % (Togan 2010).

For short-term reliefs, the Turkish government implemented stimulus packages that represented an estimated 0.83 % in 2008, 2.17 % in 2009, and 2.15 % in 2010 as a ratio of GDP. The first package, announced in October 2008, mainly related to labor markets. In 2009, further stimulus measures were introduced, including supports to small and medium-sized enterprises (SMEs) engaged in export (Babacan 2009; ILO 2010b). Additional resources were also allocated for infrastructure and irrigation projects and roads, and transfers to local administrations were increased significantly. An allocation of US$367 million (TRY551 million) was earmarked for these programs to be spent by the end of 2009, and US$339 million (TRY509 million) for 2010. In February 2009, the short-time work period was extended to a maximum of 6 months for the years 2008, 2009, and 2010. The amount of short-time work payments was increased by 50 % (ILO 2010b). In addition, Turkish government announced a new and quite comprehensive investment incentive scheme including reductions in corporate income taxes, lower employment taxes, and allocations of Treasury-owned land for investments made before the end of 2010 (Togan 2010). Readers can refer to Appendix 1 for the details of 2008 and 2009 stimulus packages.

According to Turkish policy makers, there was no need to increase government expenditures, assuming that the world economy would recover toward the end of 2009 and Turkish exports would increase (Togan 2010). Domestic demand, which had contracted in tandem with deteriorating business and lending conditions, would also increase in parallel with the improvements in the world economy. Thus, under the policies announced in the Medium Term Program, Turkey would be moving toward attaining internal balance without having to increase public expenditures (Togan 2010).

In Turkey, although the recovery in the real economy was gradual, the financial markets started to recover in the second quarter of 2009 (Yorukoglu and Atasoy 2012). Unlike many economies, Turkish financial institutions have not required any capital support. In fact, the average capital adequacy ratio in the Turkish banking sector rose during the 2001 crisis, fluctuating at around 20 %, well above the target level of 12 % and the legally required level of 8 %. The profitability of Turkish banks actually increased in 2008 and 2009, and Turkey is one of the few countries whose credit rating has improved significantly during the crisis (Yorukoglu and Atasoy 2012). The 6 % growth rate recorded in the fourth quarter of 2009 compared to a year earlier indicates that the Turkish economy has started to emerge from the crisis (ILO 2010b).

Chapter 3
National Intellectual Capital Development in the Four Countries

In this chapter, we first present the development of national intellectual capital (NIC) in the four countries over 6 years, then graphically display the relationship between each individual capital with GDP per capita (ppp). Afterward, we describe the relative position of long- and short-term intellectual capital in these four economies and explain the dynamics of NIC in three time periods (2005–2006, 2007–2008, and 2009–2010). Finally, we illustrate the NIC trajectory of these four economies on three-dimensional (3D) 48-country landscapes.

National Intellectual Capital Development

National intellectual capital measurement model in this study is based on the indicators described in Appendix 3, containing human capital, market capital, process capital, renewal capital, and financial capital. This model has been statistically proven for validity and reliability. The definitions of the indicators are listed in Appendix 4. This booklet series covers a total of 48 countries in 11 country clusters, details of which are provided in Appendix 5.

For a full picture of the 48 countries being studied, Appendix 6 contains the scores and rankings of human capital, market capital, process capital, renewal capital, financial capital, and overall NIC covered in this booklet series. Table 3.1 summarizes the status of the four countries out of the 48 countries reported in Appendix 6. For NIC ranking, Israel is 6th among the 48 countries, followed by Jordan at 33rd, Turkey at 36th, and South Africa at 37th. Israel excels in human capital and renewal capital, both ranking fourth, however, its financial capital ranked only 24th.

The following six figures compare human capital, market capital, process capital, renewal capital, financial capital, and NIC of the four countries, respectively. All the individual capital scores are based on 1–10 scale and the score of NIC is the sum of the five capital scores.

C. Y.-Y. Lin et al., *National Intellectual Capital and the Financial Crisis in Israel, Jordan, South Africa, and Turkey*, SpringerBriefs in Economics,
DOI: 10.1007/978-1-4614-7981-9_3,

Table 3.1 National intellectual capital scores and ranking of Israel, Jordan, South Africa, and Turkey among 48 countries spanning 2005–2010

Country	Human capital		Market capital		Process capital		Renewal capital		Financial capital		NIC	
	Score	Ranking	Score	Ranking	Score	Ranking	Score	Ranking	Score	Ranking	Score	Ranking
Israel	8.040	4	5.954	16	6.454	17	7.091	4	9.414	24	36.953	6
Jordan	5.345	37	5.341	26	4.411	32	2.212	30	7.865	45	25.174	33
South Africa	4.708	45	4.976	30	4.472	31	1.677	39	8.472	41	24.306	37
Turkey	4.703	46	5.227	27	4.167	34	1.666	40	8.690	36	24.453	36

Human Capital

National human capital mainly represents a nation's investment in nurturing qualified human resources, such as higher education enrollment, skilled labor, and public expenditure on education. It is a long-term-oriented NIC (Lin and Edvinsson 2011: 323), taking time to develop yet not susceptible to external impact. Figure 3.1 shows that human capital of these four countries is relatively stable over the studied 6 years, with Israel consistently having the highest human capital, far above the other three countries. Jordan's human capital is a little better than that of South Africa's and Turkey's. Jordan and Turkey increased their human capital after the financial crisis (2009 and 2010).

Market Capital

National market capital mainly represents international trade and relationships, such as cross-border ventures, globalization, and exports of goods. Figure 3.2 shows that Israel and Jordan had market capital decrease in 2008, with Israel bouncing back in 2009 while Jordan continued to slide. Comparing 2010 market capital with that of 2005, Israel's and Turkey's scores improved; however, Jordan's and South Africa's declined. Market capitals for these four countries are not too far apart from each other in this figure.

Fig. 3.1 Human capital of Israel, Jordan, South Africa, and Turkey

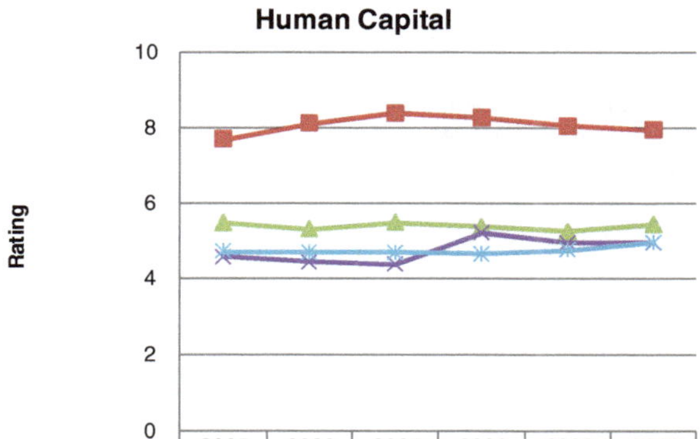

	2005	2006	2007	2008	2009	2010
Israel	7.66	8.08	8.35	8.23	8.01	7.91
Jordan	5.43	5.27	5.44	5.32	5.20	5.40
South Africa	4.52	4.39	4.34	5.18	4.91	4.91
Turkey	4.68	4.65	4.64	4.61	4.72	4.91

Fig. 3.2 Market capital of Israel, Jordan, South Africa, and Turkey

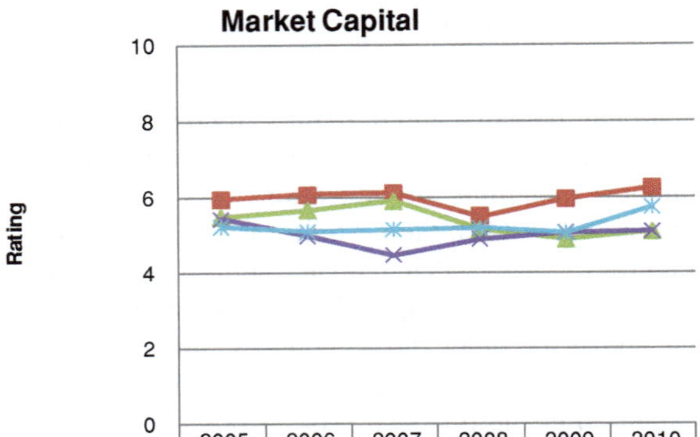

	2005	2006	2007	2008	2009	2010
Israel	5.93	6.05	6.09	5.49	5.93	6.23
Jordan	5.47	5.65	5.88	5.11	4.86	5.07
South Africa	5.41	4.96	4.46	4.88	5.06	5.08
Turkey	5.22	5.08	5.14	5.17	5.04	5.72

Process Capital

National process capital represents the infrastructure required for building a prosperous society, such as capital availability, mobile phone subscribers, and government efficiency. Figure 3.3 shows that Israel had the largest scale decline and Jordan experienced a moderate decline of process capital in 2008. Israel bounced back quickly while Jordan continued its decline in 2009. South Africa and Turkey did not have much change in process capital between 2008 and 2009. However, South Africa's process capital kept on rising and Turkey's declined a little in 2010. Over the 6 years, Israel consistently had the highest level of process capital of this cluster.

Fig. 3.3 Process capital of Israel, Jordan, South Africa, and Turkey

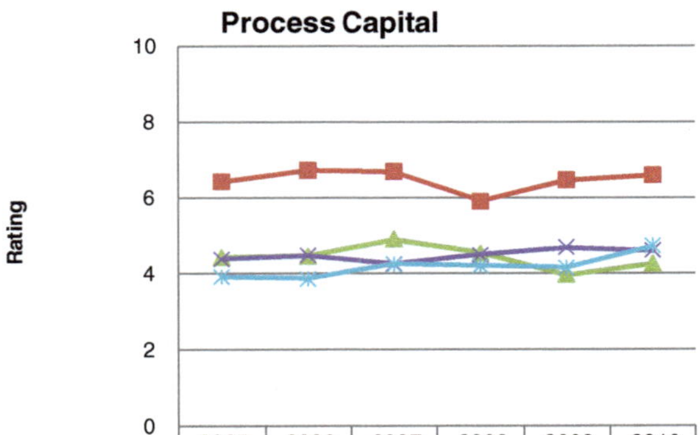

	2005	2006	2007	2008	2009	2010
Israel	6.41	6.71	6.68	5.89	6.46	6.58
Jordan	4.41	4.44	4.89	4.51	3.96	4.25
South Africa	4.37	4.47	4.24	4.48	4.68	4.60
Turkey	3.90	3.84	4.22	4.19	4.14	4.72

Renewal Capital

National renewal capital represents the capability of R&D and innovation, such as R&D spending, scientific articles, and patents. Figure 3.4 shows that Israel consistently had much higher renewal capital than the other three countries over the years examined. Its renewal capital greatly improved in 2009, however declined a little in 2010. Jordan's renewal capital increased markedly in 2008, yet plummeted in 2009. In South Africa and Turkey, little change was experienced over the years, despite their low levels.

Financial Capital

Financial capital is the GDP per capita (PPP) in US dollars converted into a score from 1 to 10. The process of score conversion is explained in Appendix 3. Figure 3.5 shows that the relative position of the four countries does not change over the 6 years. Israel has the highest financial capital, followed by Turkey, South Africa, and Jordan. In real dollars, the average GDP per capita (PPP) from 2005–2010 is US$27,430 for Israel, US$5,125 for Jordan, US$9,871 for South Africa, and US$12,511 for Turkey.

The above analyses reveal that Jordan generally has the lowest score in various capitals (except human capital), its financial capital is also the lowest among the four countries. Israel excels in every capital score, compared to the other three countries and has the highest financial capital.

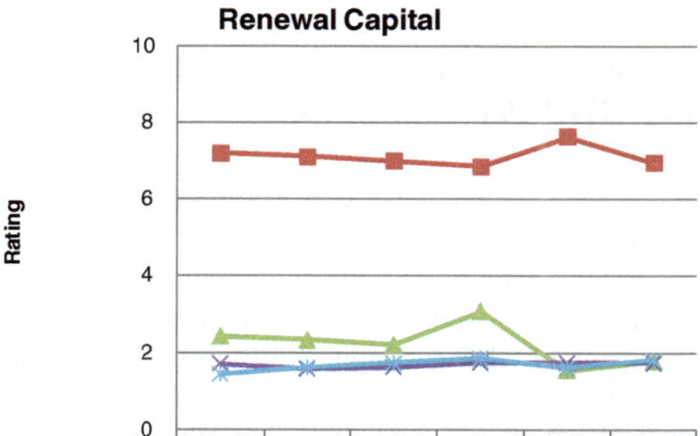

	2005	2006	2007	2008	2009	2010
Israel	7.16	7.07	6.97	6.82	7.61	6.93
Jordan	2.41	2.31	2.19	3.06	1.53	1.76
South Africa	1.70	1.57	1.61	1.73	1.73	1.72
Turkey	1.43	1.60	1.71	1.84	1.60	1.81

Fig. 3.4 Renewal capital of Israel, Jordan, South Africa, and Turkey

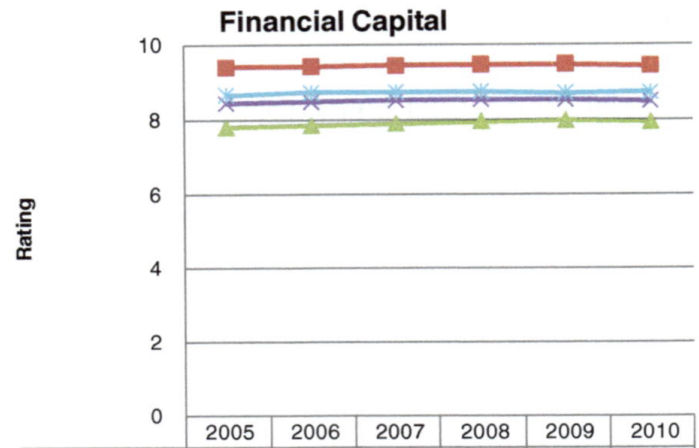

	2005	2006	2007	2008	2009	2010
Israel	9.37	9.40	9.41	9.44	9.45	9.41
Jordan	7.77	7.81	7.86	7.92	7.94	7.89
South Africa	8.42	8.45	8.49	8.51	8.50	8.46
Turkey	8.64	8.69	8.72	8.72	8.68	8.69

Fig. 3.5 Financial capital of Israel, Jordan, South Africa, and Turkey

NIC

NIC is the overall national intellectual capital containing the above five types of capital. Figure 3.6 presents NIC trends in this cluster. In 2008, Israel's score declined with the financial crisis yet bounced back with its recovery. In addition, Israel's NIC is far ahead of the other three countries. Jordan had the second highest NIC in 2005, but then declined to fourth in 2010, with a sharp drop in 2009 after the financial crisis. South Africa had a NIC increase over the years, but was surpassed by Turkey in 2010. Turkey shows good potential in advancing its NIC in the future.

The Relationship Between Each Individual Capital and GDP Per Capita (ppp)

We investigate the relationship between each individual capital and economic growth by using the six figures (Figs. 3.7, 3.8, 3.9, 3.10, 3.11, and 3.12). The graphs have four dimensions, the *X*-axis changes from graph to graph (NIC, human capital, market capital, process capital, and renewal capital), the *Y*-axis is a fixed dimension of GDP per capita (PPP) in US dollars (named GDP in brief hereafter), the color shade represents renewal capital with red denoting higher levels of renewal capital, and the bubble size denoting the population of a nation. Figure 3.7 is the relationship between NIC and GDP for all 48 countries. Figures 3.8, 3.9, 3.10, 3.11, and 3.12 display the co-development of the intellectual capital-GDP relationship over the six-year timeframe for the four countries. Since financial capital is a score converted from the GDP, there is no need to plot its relationship

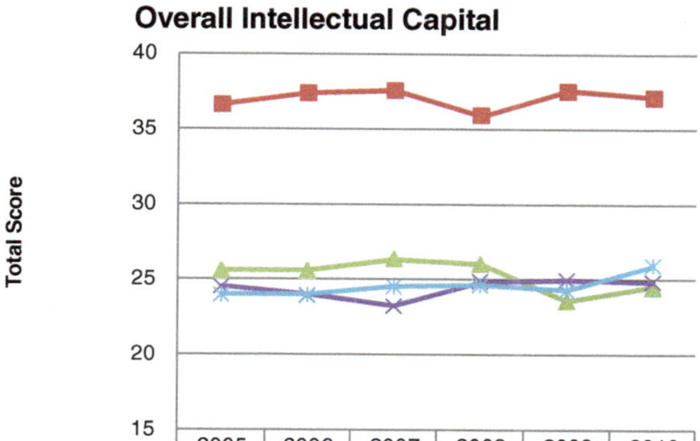

	2005	2006	2007	2008	2009	2010
Israel	36.54	37.31	37.50	35.86	37.46	37.06
Jordan	25.49	25.48	26.27	25.93	23.49	24.38
South Africa	24.42	23.84	23.14	24.78	24.88	24.77
Turkey	23.87	23.86	24.43	24.52	24.18	25.86

Fig. 3.6 NIC of Israel, Jordan, South Africa, and Turkey

with the GDP in US dollars. In the figures, 2005 is the starting point tagged with the name of the countries, and the ending point is 2010.

Figure 3.7 is particularly plotted to clearly show the full picture of the relationship between NIC and GDP for 48 countries in 2010. The strong positive correlation indicates that the higher the NIC the higher the GDP and vice versa. Consequently, enhancing NIC is definitely a strategic issue that deserves the attention of national policy makers.

With the status of all 48 countries as the background, Fig. 3.8 indicates that NIC and GDP co-development of the four countries falls in two ends of the 48-country continuum. Israel's development path is at the high end, tilted toward *X*-axis. That is, proportionally Israel's NIC is better than its GDP. In other words, Israeli NIC improvement did not correspond with GDP growth. The other three countries fall at the lower end of the continuum, with the development path of Turkey at the top of the three, South Africa in the middle, and Jordan at the lower end. In addition, Jordan's path went backward horizontally indicating NIC decline.

Figure 3.9 shows that the co-development of human capital and GDP in these countries is quite similar to that of Fig. 3.8, at two ends of the 48-country continuum. Israel's path is at the upper end tilted toward *X*-axis, indicating its human capital improvement is disproportional to its GDP growth. In addition, its human capital started to decline in 2008. The other three countries are at the lower end of the continuum, with Turkey at the top, South Africa in the middle, and Jordan at the bottom. Jordan has better human capital yet its GDP is lower than the other two countries. This figure clearly indicates that human capital in South Africa progressed significantly from 2009. Turkey has a relatively balanced development of human capital and GDP, with a diagonal progression from bottom left to upper right, albeit slowly, indicating its human capital and GDP progressed proportionally together.

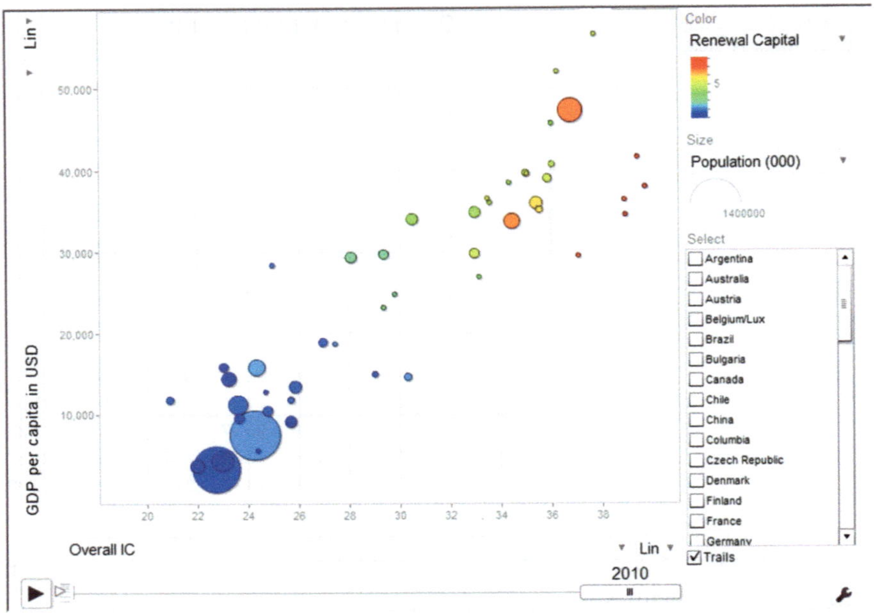

Fig. 3.7 NIC versus GDP Per Capita (PPP) for 48 countries in 2010

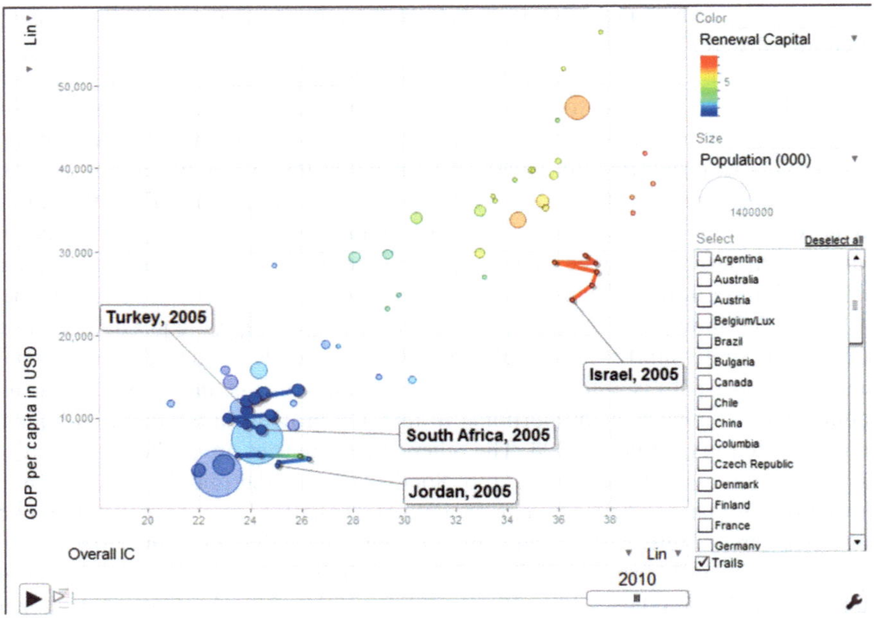

Fig. 3.8 The development of NIC and GDP per capita (PPP) for Israel, Jordan, South Africa, and Turkey from 2005 to 2010

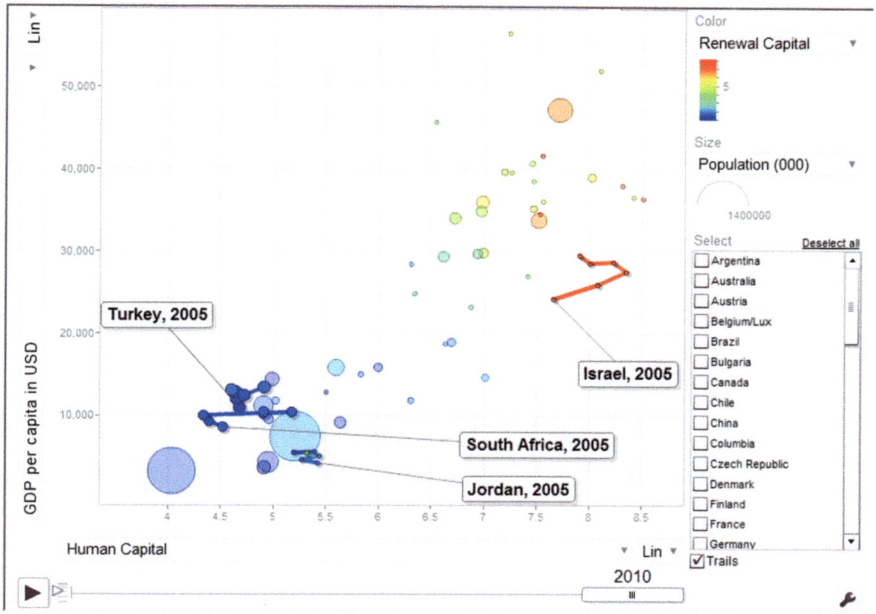

Fig. 3.9 The development of human capital and GDP per capita (PPP) for Israel, Jordan, South Africa, and Turkey from 2005 to 2010

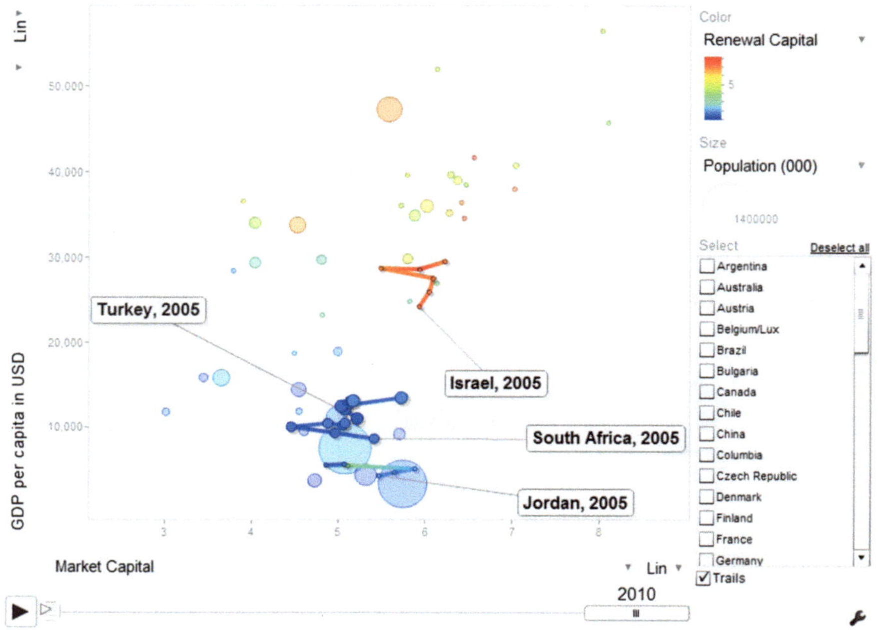

Fig. 3.10 The development of market capital and GDP per capita (PPP) for Israel, Jordan, South Africa, and Turkey from 2005 to 2010

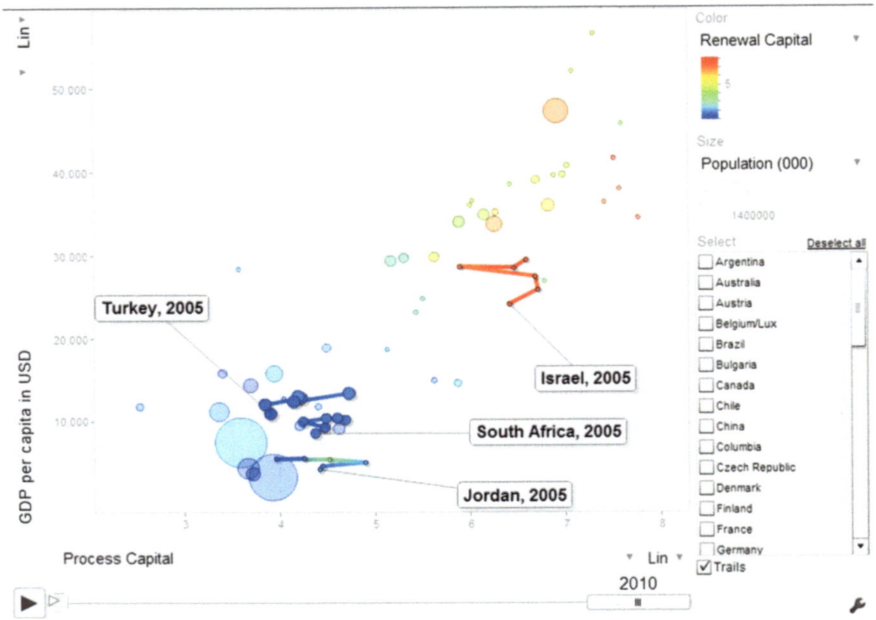

Fig. 3.11 The development of process capital and GDP per capita (PPP) for Israel, Jordan, South Africa, and Turkey from 2005 to 2010

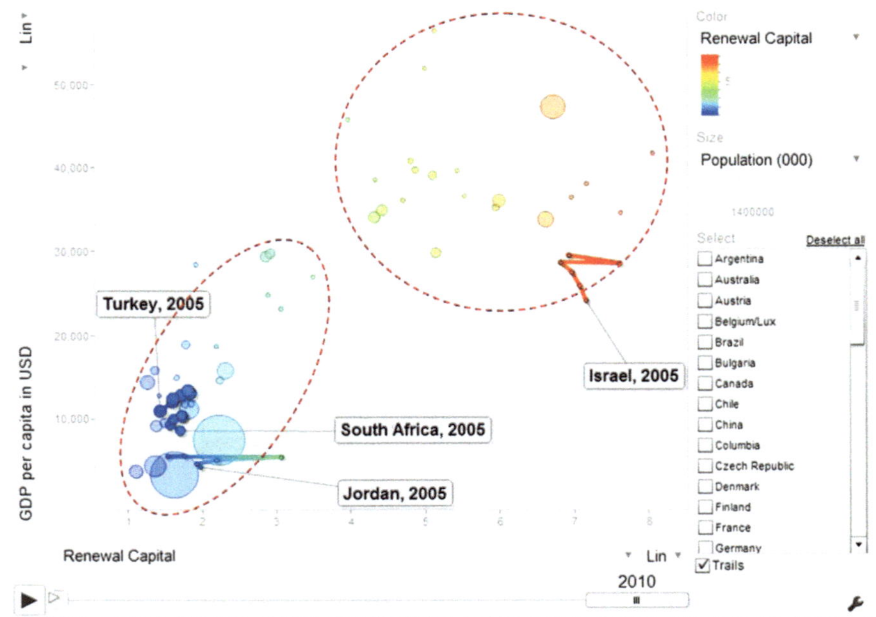

Fig. 3.12 The development of renewal capital and GDP per capita (PPP) for Israel, Jordan, South Africa, and Turkey from 2005 to 2010

In general, the bubble formation of Fig. 3.10 is very different from that of other figures in this section, without a clear belt shape continuum from the bottom left to the upper right. It means that market capital is not as highly correlated with GDP as the other capitals in this data set of 48 countries. A further explanation is that market capital of advanced countries (generally positioned at the upper right) is not necessarily better than that of emerging countries' (the two big bubbles at the bottom center are China and India).

Path development of the four countries is largely located in the middle part of *X*-axis with three different levels of GDP. Israel is in the upper bound, Turkey and South Africa in the middle, and Jordan at the lower bound. The path of Israel went backwards during the financial crisis, then bounced back after the crisis. Jordan and South Africa clearly had declining market capital after the financial crisis. On the contrary, Turkey advanced its market capital post-crisis.

In Fig. 3.11, the belt shape continuum appears again, indicating that process capital is highly correlated with GDP in this set of data. The path development of the four countries is again at the two ends of the continuum, with Israel in the middle upper end and the other three countries at the lower end. Turkey is at the upper bound among the three, South Africa in the middle, and Jordan at the bottom. Israel's process capital declined during the financial crisis, yet bounced back after the financial crisis. Jordan's process capital declined starting in 2007; however, South Africa's and Turkey's advanced over the years.

Figure 3.12 indicates that renewal capital and GDP co-development of the 48 countries has two formations. The spreading formation for the advanced countries at the upper right, and the belt shape continuum for the less developed countries at the bottom left. This means, for advanced countries, higher renewal capital does not necessarily correlate with higher GDP and vice versa. Yet, for less developed countries, increases in renewal capital do explain higher GDP. From the formation of the bottom left continuum, it is clear that small increases in renewal capital were accompanied with relatively high GDP growth. This finding reveals a strong message that investing in renewal capital development may bring better GDP growth for less developed countries.

Israel's renewal capital and GDP co-development is at the upper right circle, tilted toward *X*-axis (renewal capital), whereas that of the other three countries is grouped at the bottom left continuum. Jordan's renewal capital went backwards after the financial crisis with little progress in GDP (horizontal path). The path of both South Africa and Turkey indicated relatively balanced development of renewal capital and GDP, although the range is small.

Long-Term and Short-Term National Intellectual Capital

In addition to the above six figures that exhibit the relationship of each individual capital with GDP, the four figures (Figs. 3.13, 3.14, 3.15, 3.16) further plot the relationships between human capital and renewal capital as well as between

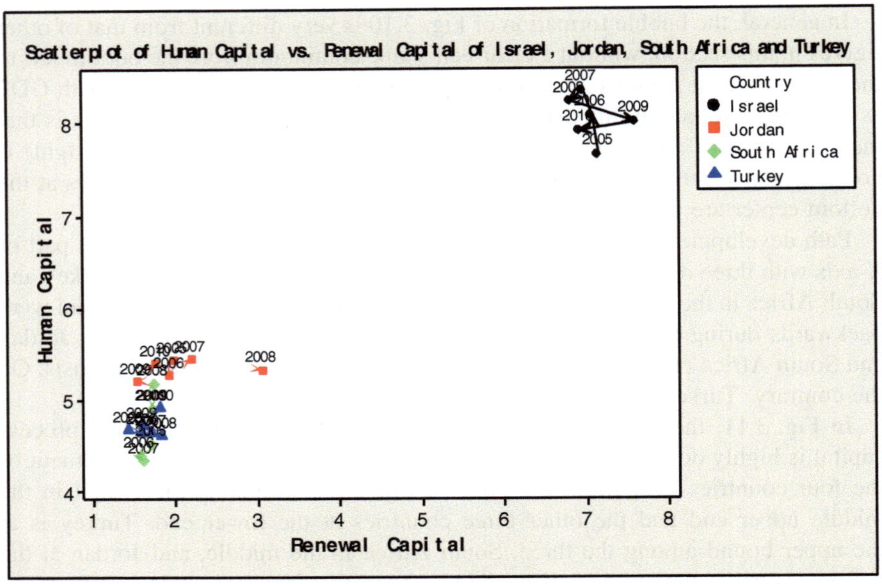

Fig. 3.13 Scatterplot of human capital versus renewal capital for Israel, Jordan, South Africa, and Turkey

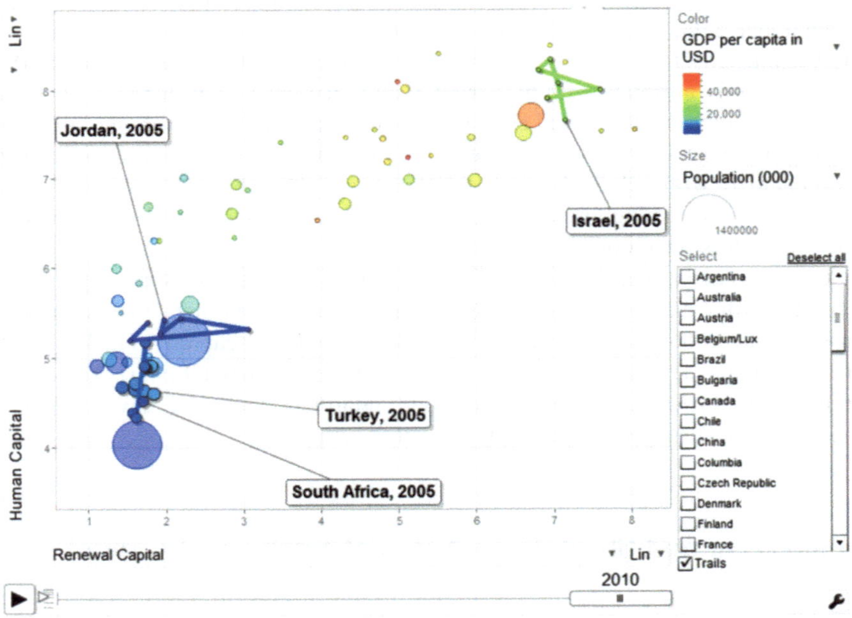

Fig. 3.14 Human capital versus renewal capital for Israel, Jordan, South Africa, and Turkey

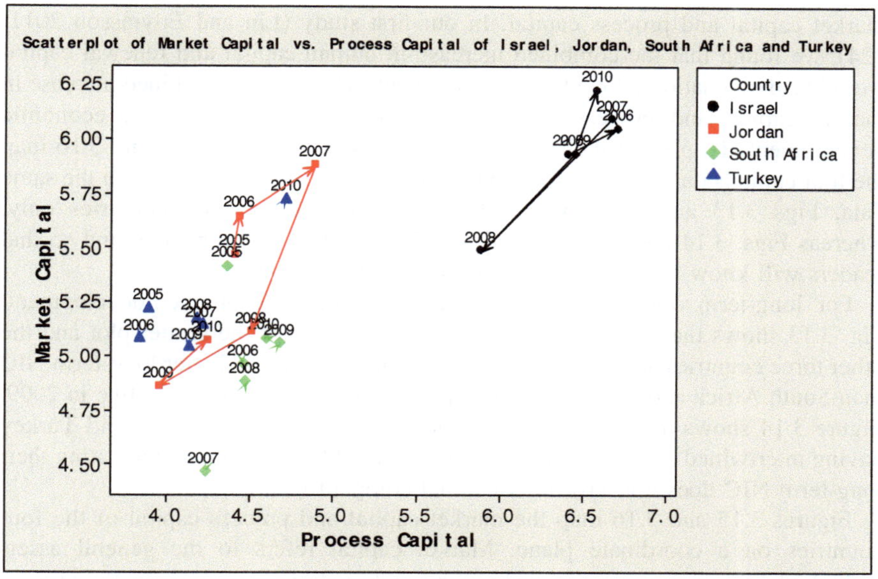

Fig. 3.15 Scatterplot of market capital versus process capital of Israel, Jordan, South Africa, and Turkey

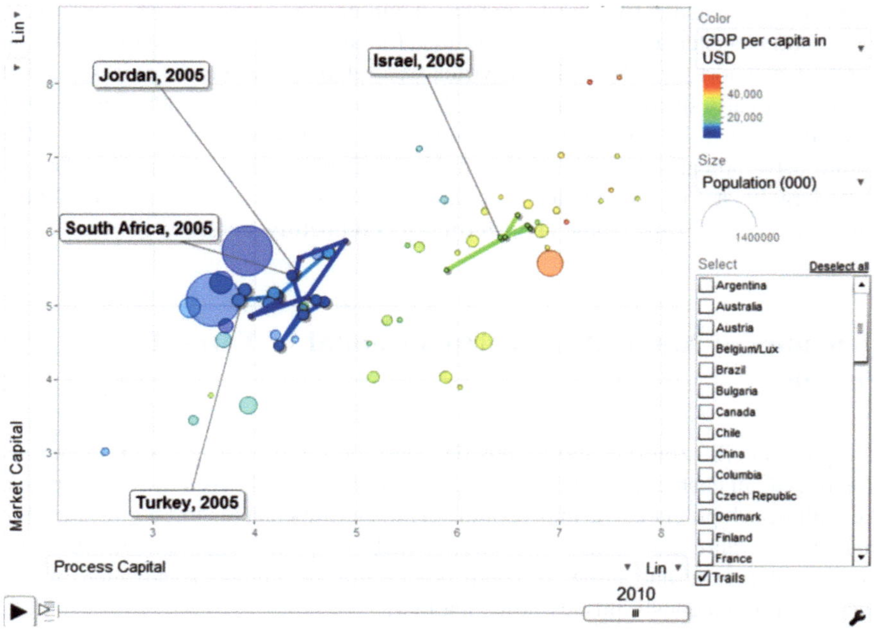

Fig. 3.16 Market capital versus process capital of Israel, Jordan, South Africa, and Turkey

market capital and process capital. In our first study (Lin and Edvinsson 2011: 324), we found that the combined increase in human capital and renewal capital would lead to a nation's long term development; whereas the combined increase in market capital and process capital will result in more immediate economic development. To present their relationships, Figs. 3.13, 3.14, 3.15, and 3.16 map the four capitals on a coordinate with two types of presentation. Based on the same data, Figs. 3.13 and 3.15 exhibit the scatterplot for the four countries only, whereas Figs. 3.14 and 3.16 show all the 48 countries as the background so that readers will know the relative positions of these four countries.

For long-term oriented human capital and renewal capital co-development, Fig. 3.13 shows that Israel is in the upper right corner of the scatter plot and the other three countries are in the bottom left corner. Jordan had better long-term NIC than South Africa and Turkey initially, yet it experienced a sharp decline in 2009. Figure 3.14 shows a clear 48-country continuum, with South Africa and Turkey having intertwined development at the lower end of the continuum, indicating their long-term NIC does not have international competitiveness.

Figures 3.15 and 3.16 map the market capital and process capital of the four countries on a coordinate plane. Market capital refers to the general assets embodied in a nation's relationship with international markets while process capital refers to the national infrastructure. For short-term competition, these are the two types of capital that can be expected to produce faster results if a nation is willing to engage in more extensive investments.

Figures 3.15 and 3.16 indicate that Israel still had the highest short-term NIC in this country cluster. Figure 3.15 shows that Jordan declined sharply from 2007 in terms of its short-term NIC. South Africa was relatively strong in process capital and had an early decline starting in 2006, yet bounced back in 2008. Turkey was relatively strong in short-term NIC and had a continuous growth since 2006. Figure 3.16 indicates that the short-term NIC of Jordan, South Africa, and Turkey were largely at the middle range among the 48 countries. That is, these three emerging countries had some short-term NIC competitiveness.

Dynamics of National Intellectual Capital in Three Time Periods

The previous illustrations and graphs describe the internal progression or regression of NIC in each country with individual capital score changes over 6 years and the path development of various capitals. The ranking changes to be introduced in this section represent external or international competitiveness among 48 countries. Ranking, by and large, is a zero-sum game in which the advance of one country simultaneously pushes down another.

In order to probe the dynamics of NIC change before and after the financial crisis, we plotted Figs. 3.17, 3.18, 3.19, 3.20, 3.21, 3.22, 3.23, 3.24, and Table 3.2

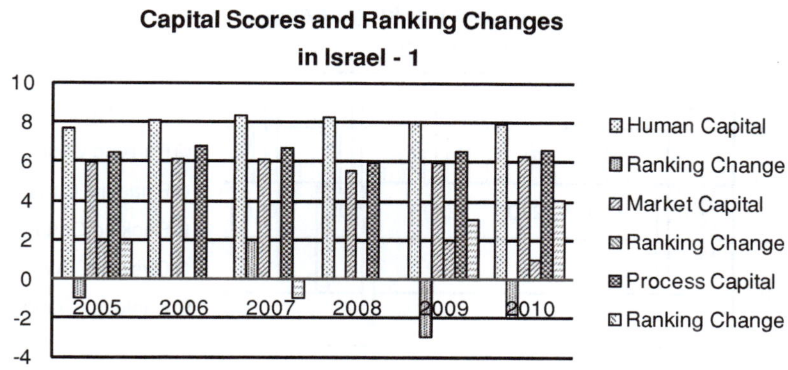

Fig. 3.17 Human capital, market capital, process capital, and ranking changes in Israel

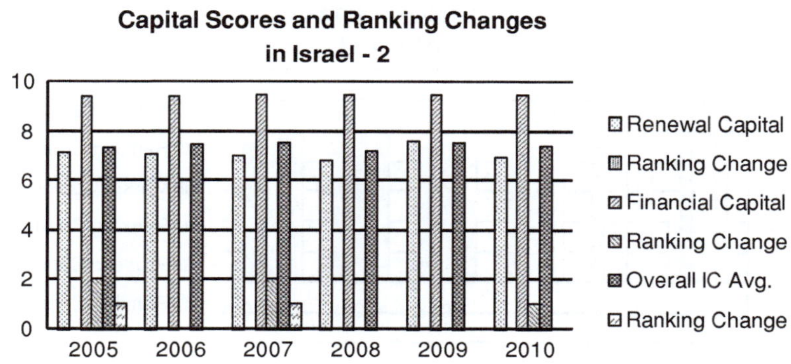

Fig. 3.18 Renewal capital, financial capital, average NIC, and ranking changes in Israel

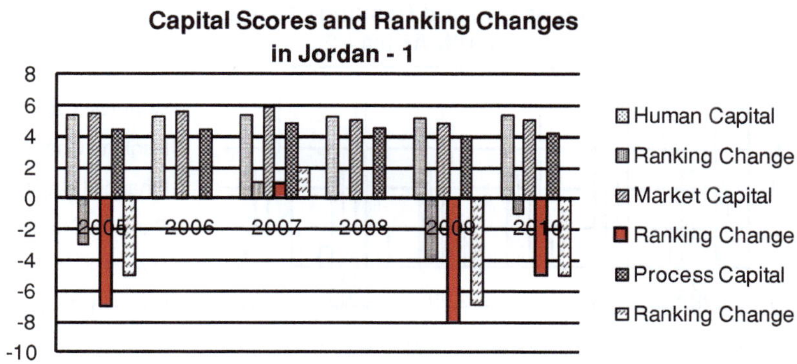

Fig. 3.19 Human capital, market capital, process capital, and ranking changes in Jordan

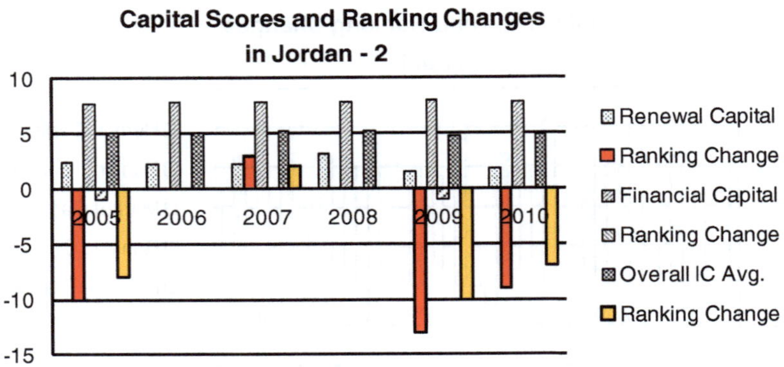

Fig. 3.20 Renewal capital, financial capital, average NIC, and ranking changes in Jordan

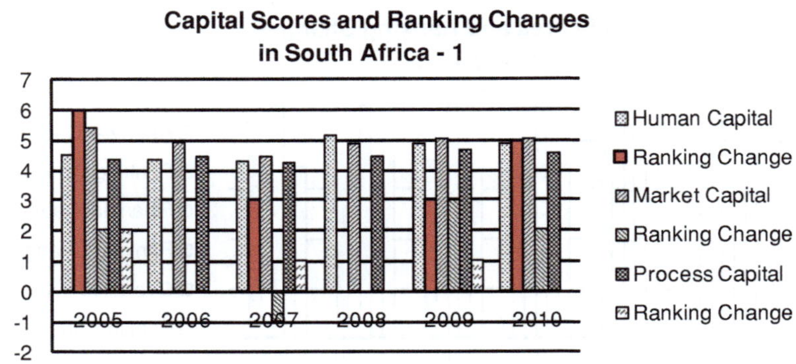

Fig. 3.21 Human capital, market capital, process capital, and ranking changes in South Africa

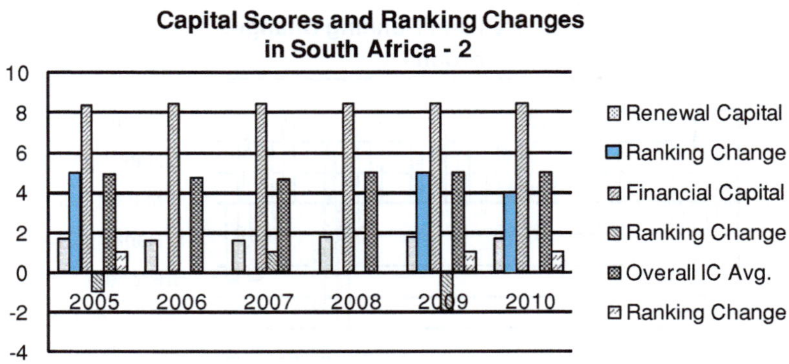

Fig. 3.22 Renewal capital, financial capital, average NIC, and ranking changes in South Africa

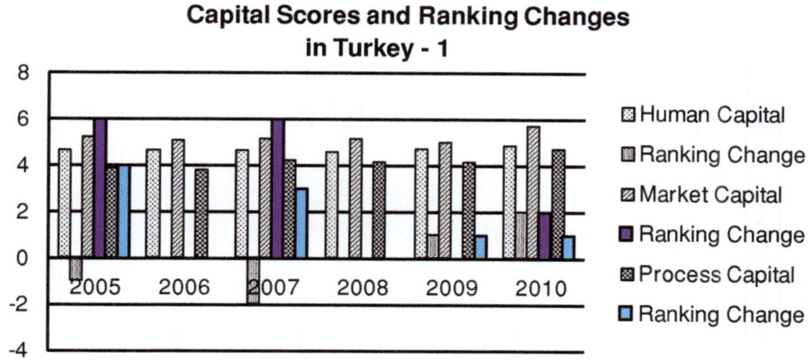

Fig. 3.23 Human capital, market capital, process capital, and ranking changes in Turkey

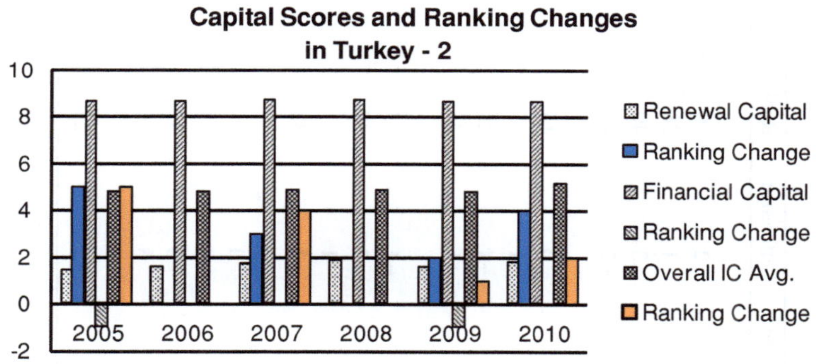

Fig. 3.24 Renewal capital, financial capital, average NIC, and ranking changes in Turkey

in three time periods: 2005–2006, 2007–2008, and 2009–2010. To have a clearer presentation, we separate the data in two sets. The first set contains capital scores and ranking changes of human capital, market capital, and process capital in Figs. 3.17, 3.19, 3.21, and 3.23. The second set exhibits capital scores and ranking changes of renewal capital, financial capital, and average NIC in Figs. 3.18, 3.20, 3.22, and 3.24.

The figures are mapped based on the mean capital scores and ranking changes of each period. Ranking change in Figs. 3.17, 3.18, 3.19, 3.20, 3.21, 3.22, 3.23, and 3.24 is next to each capital score and copied from the bold-faced ranking difference of columns 2, 5, 7, and 9 of Table 3.2. Using the human capital ranking difference of Israel (−1, 2, −3, −2) as example, ranking change "−1" representing the difference between the third (2009–2010) and first (2005–2006) period is plotted at the year 2005; ranking change "2" representing the difference between the second period (2007–2008) and first (2005–2006) is plotted at the year 2007; ranking change "−3" representing the difference between the third period (2009–2010) and second (2007–2008) is plotted at year 2009; and ranking change

Table 3.2 Ranking changes in three time periods for Israel, Jordan, South Africa, and Turkey

	(1st–3rd period)	1st period 2005–2006	2nd period 2007–2008		3rd period 2009–2010		3rd period ranking versus overall NIC ranking	
	Difference	Ranking	Ranking	Difference	Ranking	Difference	NIC 48 ranking	Difference
Human capital								
Israel	**−1**	5	3	**2**	6	**−3**	4	**−2**
Jordan	**−3**	35	34	**1**	38	**−4**	37	**−1**
South Africa	**6**	46	43	**3**	40	**3**	45	**5**
Turkey	**−1**	43	45	**−2**	44	**1**	46	**2**
Market capital								
Israel	**2**	17	17	**0**	15	**2**	16	**1**
Jordan	**−7**	24	23	**1**	31	**−8**	26	**−5**
South Africa	**2**	30	31	**−1**	28	**3**	30	**2**
Turkey	**6**	31	25	**6**	25	**0**	27	**2**
Process capital								
Israel	**2**	15	16	**−1**	13	**3**	17	**4**
Jordan	**−5**	32	30	**2**	37	**−7**	32	**−5**
South Africa	**2**	33	32	**1**	31	**1**	31	**0**
Turkey	**4**	37	34	**3**	33	**1**	34	**1**
Renewal capital								
Israel	**0**	4	4	**0**	4	**0**	4	**0**
Jordan	**−10**	29	26	**3**	39	**−13**	30	**−9**
South Africa	**5**	40	40	**0**	35	**5**	39	**4**
Turkey	**5**	41	38	**3**	36	**2**	40	**4**
Financial capital								
Israel	**2**	25	23	**2**	23	**0**	24	**1**

(continued)

Table 3.2 (continued)

	(1st–3rd period)	1st period 2005–2006	2nd period 2007–2008		3rd period 2009–2010		3rd period ranking versus overall NIC ranking	
	Difference	Ranking	Ranking	Difference	Ranking	Difference	NIC 48 ranking	Difference
Jordan	**−1**	44	44	**0**	45	**−1**	45	**0**
South Africa	**−1**	40	39	**1**	41	**−2**	41	**0**
Turkey	**−1**	35	35	**0**	36	**−1**	36	**0**
NIC								
Israel	**1**	7	6	**1**	6	**0**	6	**0**
Jordan	**−8**	32	30	**2**	40	**−10**	33	**−7**
South Africa	**1**	37	37	**0**	36	**1**	37	**1**
Turkey	**5**	39	35	**4**	34	**1**	36	**2**

Remarks

1. The second column compares the third (2009–2010) period ranking with the 1st (2005–2006) period ranking
2. The fifth column compares the second (2007–2008) period ranking with the 1st (2005–2006) period ranking
3. The seventh column compares the third (2009–2010) period ranking with the second (2007–2008) period ranking
4. The last column compares the most current third period ranking (2009–2010) with the original six-year average NIC48 ranking summarized in Table 3.2

"−2" representing the difference between the third period (2009–2010) and 6-year average ranking (exhibited in Table 3.1) is plotted at the year 2010. Special attention can be paid to the negative numbers, which means that the level of a particular capital is higher before than after the financial crisis. Since it is easier to read figures than tables, we will describe the finding of each figure one by one.

From Fig. 3.17 and Table 3.2, Israeli human capital had the largest ranking decline (−1, 2, −3, −2), especially the −3 and −2 ranking loss when comparing the most recent 2009–2010 with 2007–2008 and with the 6-year average. That is, its human capital decreased after the financial crisis. However, its market capital gained international competitiveness after the crisis with positive ranking changes (2, 0, 2, 1). Its process capital mainly gained international competitiveness with ranking changes of (2, −1, 3, 4); its 2009–2010 ranking surpasses the 6 years average by four ranks. A quick view of Fig. 3.17 shows four negative numbers, ranging from −1 to −3.

Figure 3.18 and Table 3.2 indicate that Israel did not have any ranking change in renewal capital (0, 0, 0, 0). Its financial capital (2, 2, 0, 1) and NIC (1, 1, 0, 0) gained ranks after the financial crisis. A quick view of Fig. 3.18 shows no negative number at all. In general, Israel gained international competitiveness in various capitals, except human capital.

Figure 3.19 and Table 3.2 show that Jordan's bar charts are very different from those of Israel, with quite a few large negative numbers. Jordan's ranking changes of human capital (−3, 1, −4, −1), market capital (−7, 1, −8, −5), and process capital (−5, 2, −7, −5) represent that the country was losing international competitiveness in these three types of capital after the financial crisis.

Figure 3.20 and Table 3.2 indicate a similar situation as Figure 3.19. Jordan's ranking changes of renewal capital (−10, 3, −13, −9), financial capital (−1, 0, −1, 0), and NIC (−8, 2, −10, −7) show an even larger scale of losing international competitiveness after the financial crisis. The situation is particularly serious in renewal capital.

These findings coincide with Jordan's losing global competitiveness with GCI ranking dropped from 45 to 71 in 7 years (Fig. 1.1). These two figures manifest the value of ranking change comparison presented in this section. Although Figs. 3.8, 3.9, 3.10, 3.11, and 3.12 showed the declines of Jordan's various capitals, we did not know that the country was losing its international competitiveness in intangible assets on such a large scale after the financial crisis until this ranking change analysis.

Figure 3.21 and Table 3.2 show the ranking changes of human capital (6, 3, 3, 5), market capital (2, −1, 3, 2), and process capital (2, 1, 1, 0) for South Africa. A quick view of Fig. 3.21 indicates one small negative number only. This means, South Africa was generally gaining international competitiveness in these three types of capital after the financial crisis. Its human capital progress is particularly noticeable with a good sign for the country. Since human capital is a long-term oriented NIC, it is not likely to change much once obtained.

Figure 3.22 and Table 3.2 indicate South Africa's ranking changes of renewal capital (5, 0, 5, 4), financial capital (−1, 1, −2, 0), and NIC (1, 0, 1, 1). A quick view of Fig. 3.22 indicates two small negative numbers only. Its gaining international competitiveness in renewal capital after the financial crisis is an especially encouraging sign. Its improvement in both renewal capital and human capital ranking casts a promising prospect for the country's future development.

Figure 3.23 and Table 3.2 show the ranking changes of human capital (−1, −2, 1, 2), market capital (6, 6, 0, 2), and process capital (4, 3, 1, 1) for Turkey. The first number of market capital (6) and process capital (4) means Turkey was gaining international competitiveness in these two capitals after the financial crisis, comparing the period 2009–2010 and 2005–2006. A quick view of Fig. 3.23 indicates two small negative numbers only, describing Turkey's relatively good prospect especially in the short-term oriented NIC—market capital and process capital.

Figure 3.24 and Table 3.2 indicate Turkey's ranking changes of renewal capital (5, 3, 2, 4), financial capital (−1, 0, −1, 0), and NIC (5, 4, 1, 2). A quick view of Fig. 3.24 shows two small negative numbers (−1 and −1) in financial capital only. Its gain in international competitiveness for renewal capital is an encouraging sign. Ranking gain in most of the capitals explains Turkey's improving intangible assets international competitiveness. These two figures cast relatively promising prospect for Turkey's future intangible assets development.

In summary, within this country cluster, Israel had small-scale ranking changes in various capitals, very likely due to its already high and stable NIC. For human capital, South Africa had relatively large scale ranking gains after the financial crisis. For market capital and process capital, Turkey gained the international competitiveness after the financial crisis in a relatively large scale. For renewal capital, both South Africa and Turkey had relatively large-scale ranking gains. For overall NIC, Turkey had the largest scale ranking gains after the financial crisis in this country cluster.

Among the four countries, Jordan had the largest scale ranking loss in market capital, process capital, renewal capital, and NIC after the financial crisis. Jordan's lagging NIC may partially explain its low GDP and dropping global competitiveness, as reported by the World Economic Forum.

An important finding of this section is that a small-scale internal score decrease may lead to a large scale loss of international competitiveness. An example is Jordan's renewal capital. Its 2007–2008 average renewal capital score is 2.63 and 2009–2010 average score is 1.65. With about one point decrease on a 1–10 scale, Jordan had a 13 ranking loss, which is more than a quarter in the 48-country landscape. Therefore, a country's internal progression or regression (score change) and external (international) competitiveness need to be examined together to get a fuller picture of its relative position in an international arena.

3-Dimensional National Intellectual Capital Trajectory

Up until this section, all the figures plotted different combinations of various capitals, capital-GDP co-development, and ranking changes on a flat plane. Even though Figs. 3.7, 3.8, 3.9, 3.10, 3.11, and 3.12 display four dimensions with color and bubble size as the third and fourth dimension in addition to *X*- and *Y*-axis, graphically they are still on one plane. This section presents three-dimensional (3D) graphs showing each country's NIC development trajectory on a 48-country 3D landscape of various types. Since evolution over time is always complex, combining different views from different angles may provide more comprehensive perspectives.

In what follows, we first explore the value driving context by uncovering influencing factors of GDP growth for Israel, Jordan, South Africa, and Turkey from 2005 to 2010. Second, in explaining the GDP growth, we present the high, middle and low capability which human capital, market capital, process capital and renewal capital, respectively have. Third, we examine the efficiency (GDP growth) enhancing factors and impeding factors of each country, taking each country's turning point into consideration. Last, we identify the efficiency drivers of each country in reaching a targeted GDP.

Figure 3.25 is a rectangular shape 3D landscape, with longer north–south side. The formation of the landscape is based on the data of 29 NIC indicators (presented in Appendix 3) for 48 countries covering 6 years (2005–2010), which is 8,352 (29 × 48 × 6) data points. In other words, Fig. 3.25 is the aggregated NIC landscape of the 48 countries. The rotation arrows explain that our software automatically adjusts its computer-generated images to show a better front view, right side view, or left side view according to the locations of countries we designated.

Figure 3.26 shows the rotated landscape for the reader to have a better left side view of where Israel is located. The relative NIC position of Israel is at the upper left side of the landscape. Jordan, South Africa, and Turkey (pointed out with arrows) are in the lower middle part of the landscape. The enlarged trails indicate the NIC progression (upward), regression (downward), or changing configuration (sideward) of each country over the 6 years. Each white trail on the landscape represents each country. The altitude coloring from purple, dark blue, blue, green, yellow, and red is computer generated, according to GDP values, with purple (north) representing high GDP descending to low GDP in red (south).

Figures 3.27, 3.28, and 3.29 are a set. Figure 3.27 presents four graphs indicating the high capability region of each human capital, market capital, process capital, and renewal capital in explaining the GDP growth. High capability means the data points are 20 % above the mean value of each capital. This figure shows that only the human capital, market capital, process capital, and renewal capital of Israel are in the high capability region.

Figure 3.28 displays another set of four graphs indicating the middle capability region of each human capital, market capital, process capital, and renewal capital

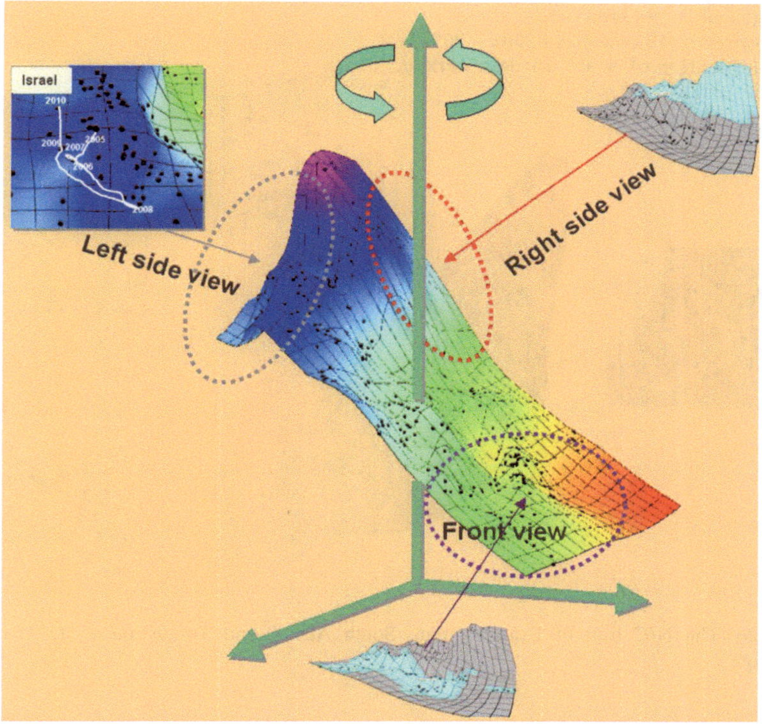

Fig. 3.25 3D 48-country landscape showing potential computer-generated rotation for a better front view, *right side* view, and *left side* view

in explaining the GDP growth. Middle capability means the data points are within the top 50 % value of each capital. This figure shows that market capital of Jordan and Turkey are positioned in the middle capability region in addition to Israel.

Figure 3.29 shows the last four graphs in this set indicating the low capability region of each human capital, market capital, process capital, and renewal capital in explaining the GDP growth. Low capability means the data points are 20 % below the mean value of each capital. This figure shows that human capital, process capital, and renewal capital of Jordan and Turkey, and all four capitals of South Africa are in the low capability region.

In general, Figs. 3.27, 3.28, and 3.29 as a set explain that Israel's NIC is in the high capability region. However, most capitals of the other three countries are in the low capability region, except the market capital of Jordan and Turkey, which are in the middle capability region. In other words, Israel can serve as a model for the other three countries in terms of NIC development.

Another set of Figs. 3.30, 3.31, 3.32, and 3.33 display efficiency enhancing or impeding factors that affect GDP growth before and after the NIC turning point for

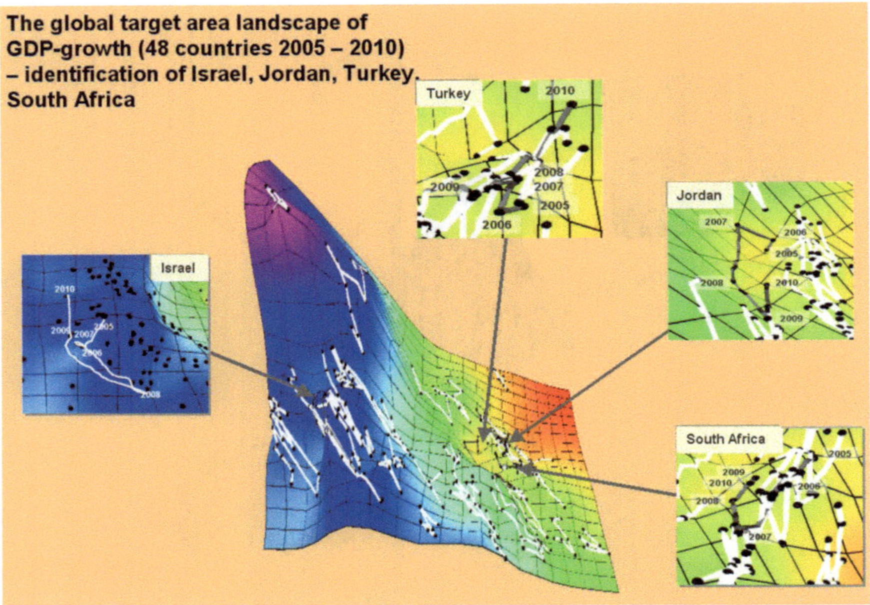

Fig. 3.26 The NIC trail of Israel, Jordan, South Africa, and Turkey on a 3D 48-country landscape

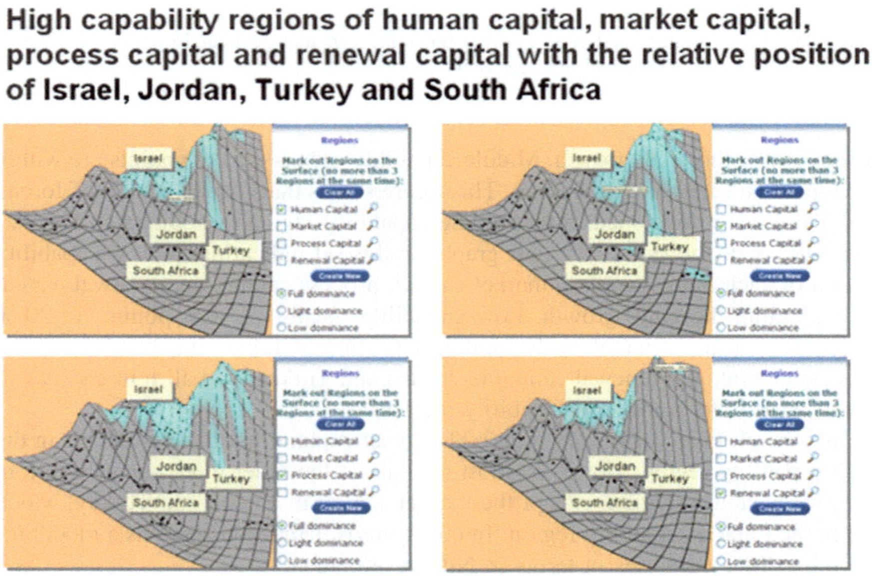

Fig. 3.27 The high capability region of human capital, market capital, process capital, and renewal capital

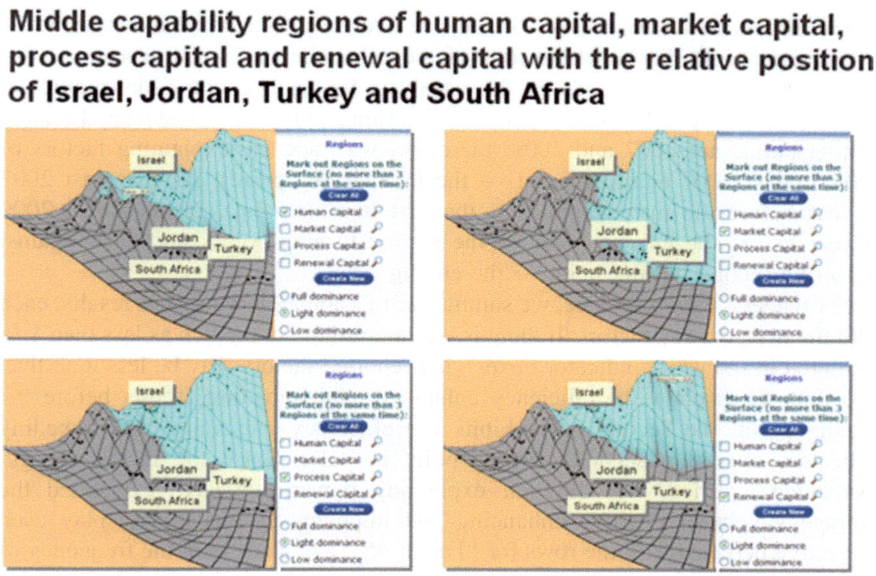

Fig. 3.28 The middle capability region of human capital, market capital, process capital, and renewal capital

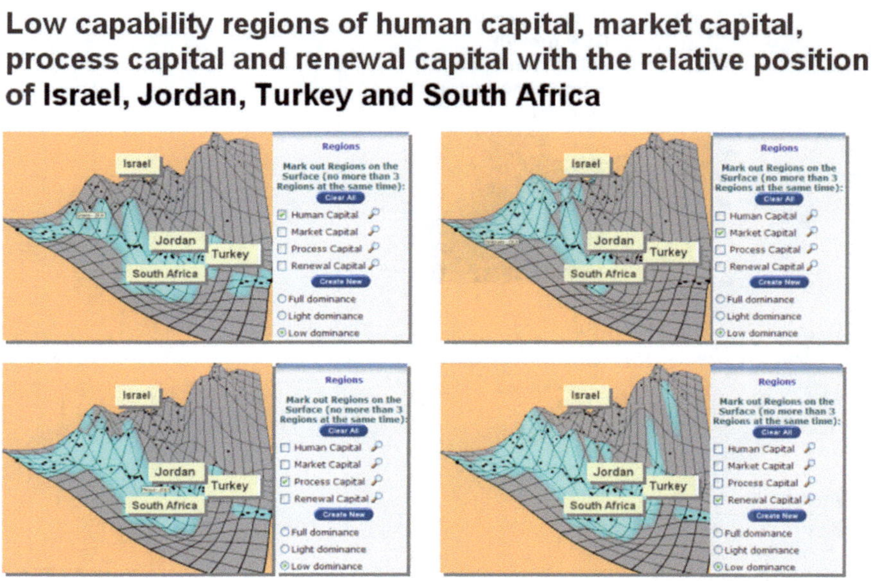

Fig. 3.29 The low capability region of human capital, market capital, process capital, and renewal capital

Israel, Jordan, South Africa, and Turkey, respectively. The white indicator boxes at the upper right display the results of the enhancing or impeding factors. We employ three or four rounds of data analysis for each country, depending on whether the country has one or two NIC turning points. For instance, Jordan's turning points are 2007 and 2009; therefore, we trace the explaining factors of 2005 against 2007 (starting point → the first turning point), 2006 against 2007 (1 year before the turning point → the first turning point), 2008 against 2009 (1 year before the turning point → the second turning point), and 2009 against 2010 (the second turning point → the ending point).

For readers' easy reference, we summarize in Table 3.3 two sets of results, each with the first five key factors. If there is a clear cutting point (such as less than 1 % exhibited in the white indicator boxes), the reported factors may be less than five. The first set displays the efficiency enhancing and impeding factors before the turning point, the second set exhibits the efficiency enhancing and impeding indicators after the (second) turning point in italic. Since the factor strength (percentage) varies with different explaining power, we have calculated the average weight of the five enhancing and impeding factors and display each respective percentage in the rows for "Factor #5". We also count the frequency of the four more frequently displayed categories, namely government related issues (G), human capital related issues (H), market capital related issues (M), and

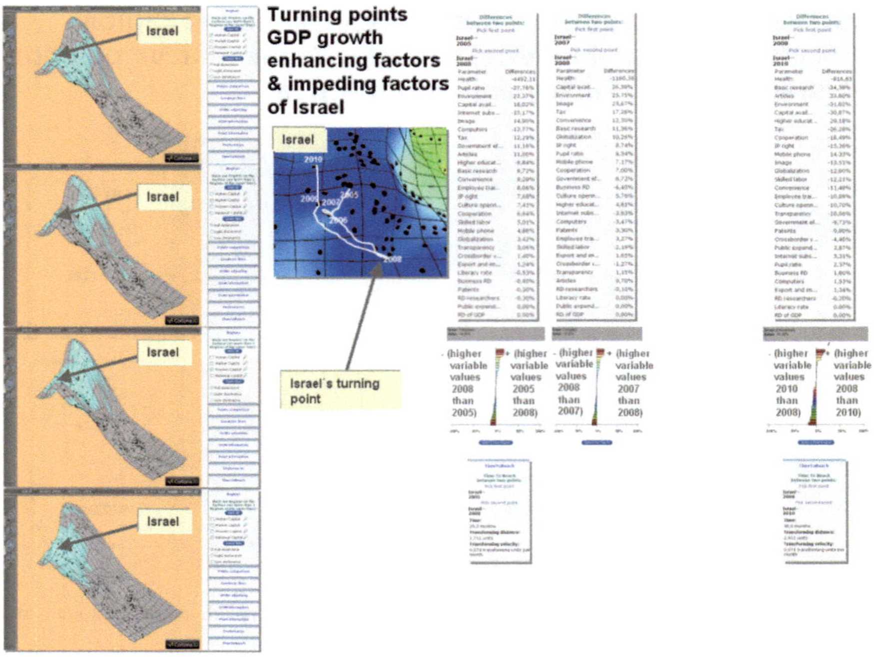

Fig. 3.30 Turning point and GDP growth enhancing and impeding factors of Israel

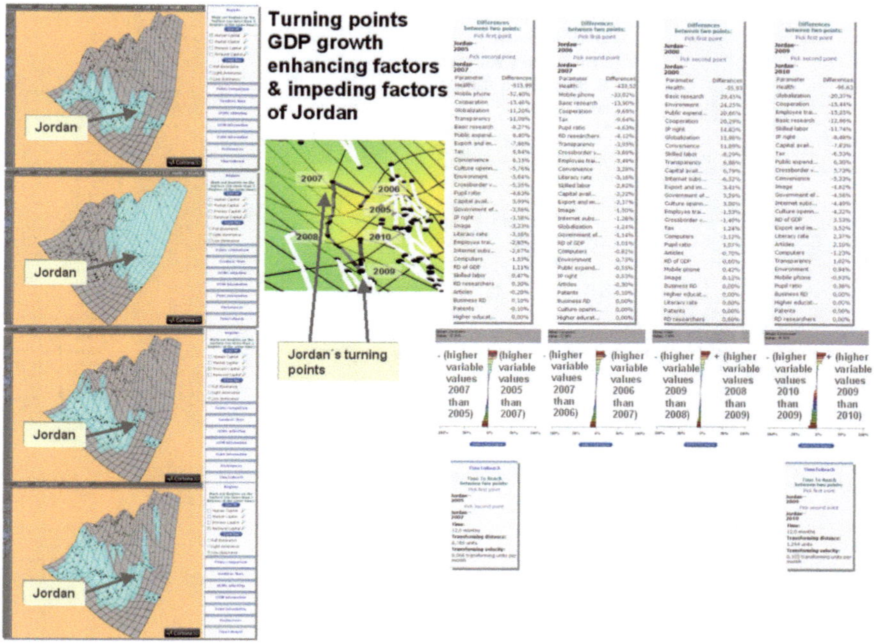

Fig. 3.31 Turning points and GDP growth enhancing and impeding factors of Jordan

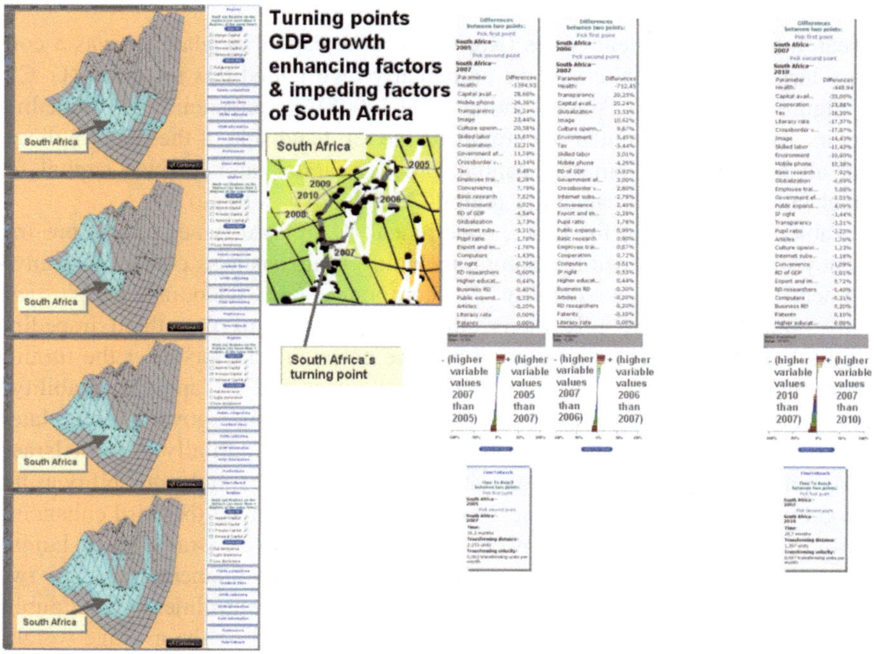

Fig. 3.32 Turning point and GDP growth enhancing and impeding factors of South Africa

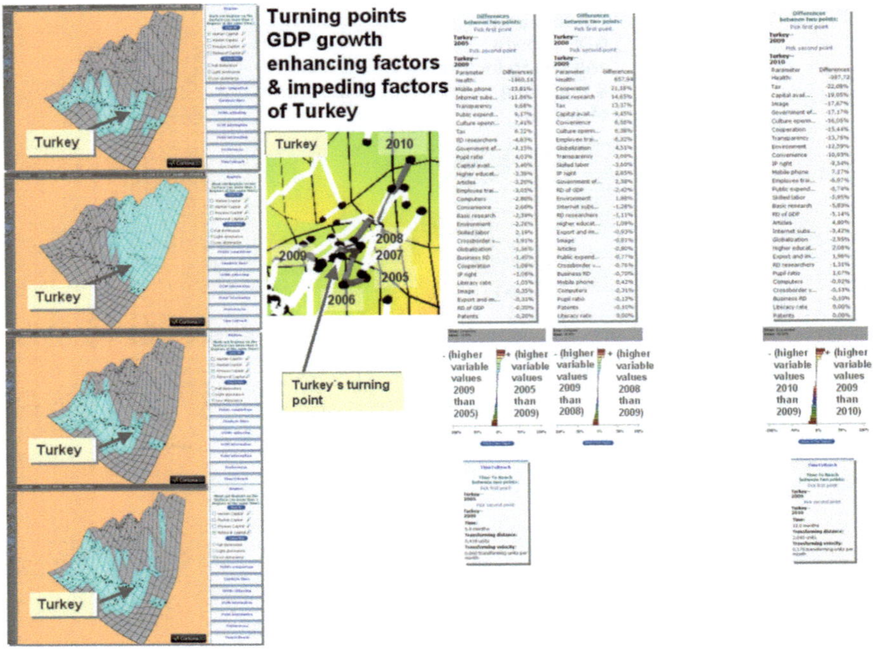

Fig. 3.33 Turning point and GDP growth enhancing and impeding factors of Turkey

research and development issues (R&D). Because capital availability was a concern during the financial crisis, we particularly highlighted this factor as "G–C".

Figure 3.30 displays Israeli turning point (2008), its enhancing and impeding factors. The four rectangular 3D graphs on the left hand side of the figure indicate that all human capital, market capital, process capital, and renewal capital for Israel fall into the high capability region (20 % above average).

Table 3.3 shows that for Israel, government (G) related issues have more frequency as the GDP impeding factors, including "fair business competition environment", "capital availability", "corporate tax encouragement" and "government efficiency". However, there are good signs that three impeding factors before the 2008 turning point became enhancing factors after the turning point, including "fair business competition environment", "capital availability" and "corporate tax encouragement". The change of three government related issues from impeding factors to enhancing factors may partially explain Israeli government's responses to arising problems. Particularly, capital availability as the second impeding factor before the 2008 turning point became the third enhancing factor after the turning point showed a good sign. However, Israel lost its human capital international competitiveness (Fig. 3.17) after the financial crisis, its two human capital related impeding factors "higher education enrollment" and "public expenditure on education" deserve some attention. Based on the average weight,

Table 3.3 Enhancing factors and impeding factors of GDP growth for Israel, Jordan, South Africa, and Turkey

Influencing factor	Israel enhancing factors	Israel impeding factors	Jordan enhancing factors	Jordan impeding factors	South Africa enhancing factors	South Africa impeding factors	Turkey enhancing factors	Turkey impeding factors
Factor #1 before (1st) turning point	Pupil-teacher ratio (H)	Fair business competition environment (G)	Mobile phone subscribers	Public expenditure on education (H)	Mobile phone subscribers	Capital availability (G–C)	Mobile phone subscribers	Transparency of government policy (G)
Factor #1 after (2nd) turning point	*Basic research* (R&D)	*Scientific articles* (R&D)	*Globalization* (M)	*Public expenditure on education* (H)	*Capital availability* (G–C)	*Mobile phone subscribers*	*Corporate tax encouragement* (G)	*Mobile phone subscribers*
Factor #2 before (1st) turning point	Internet subscribers	Capital availability (G–C)	Enterprise-university cooperation	Corporate tax encouragement (G)	R&D percentage of GDP (R&D)	Transparency of government policy (G)	Internet subscribers	Public expenditure on education (H)
Factor #2 after (2nd) turning point	*Fair business competition environment* (G)	*Higher education enrollment* (H)	*Enterprise-university cooperation*	*Cross border ventures* (M)	*Enterprise-university cooperation*	*Basic research* (R&D)	*Capital availability* (G–C)	*Scientific articles* (R&D)
Factor #3 before (1st) turning point	Computer in use per capita	Image of country (M)	Globalization (M)	Convenience of establishing new firms (G)	Internet subscribers	Image of country (M)	R&D researchers (R&D)	Openness to culture (M)
Factor #3 after (2nd) turning point	*Capital availability* (G–C)	*Mobile phone subscribers*	*Employee training* (H)	*R&D % of GDP* (R&D)	*Corporate tax encouragement* (G)	*Employee training* (H)	*Image of country* (M)	*Higher education enrollment* (H)
Factor #4 before (1st) turning point	Higher education enrollment (H)	Corporate tax encouragement (G)	Transparency of government policy (G)	Capital availability (G–C)	Export of goods (M)	Openness to culture (M)	Government efficiency (G)	Corporate tax encouragement (G)

(continued)

Table 3.3 (continued)

Influencing factor	Israel enhancing factors	Israel impeding factors	Jordan enhancing factors	Jordan impeding factors	South Africa enhancing factors	South Africa impeding factors	Turkey enhancing factors	Turkey impeding factors
Factor #4 after (2nd) turning point	*Corporate tax encouragement* (G)	*Public expenditure on education* (H)	*Basic research* (R&D)	*Export of goods* (M)	*Literacy rate* (H)	*Public expenditure on education* (H)	*Government efficiency* (G)	*Export of goods* (M)
Factor #5 before (1st) turning point	– (Average weight—16.39 %)#	Government efficiency (G) (Average weight—15.75 %)	Basic research (R&D) (Average weight—15.48 %)	R&D % of GDP (R&D) (Average weight—5.30 %)	Computers in use per capita (Average weight—7.48 %)	Skilled labor (H) (Average weight—22.91 %)	Higher education enrollment (H) (Average weight—7.61 %)	Pupil-teacher ratio (H) (Average weight—7.30 %)
Factor #5 after (2nd) turning point	*Enterprise-university cooperation* (Average weight—28.21 %)	*Internet subscribers* (Average weight—16.90 %)	*Skilled labor* (H) (Average weight—15.13 %)	*Literacy rate* (H) (Average weight—4.29 %)	*Cross border ventures* (M) (Average weight—21.92 %)	– (Average weight—4.16 %)	*Openness to culture* (M) (Average weight—18.40 %)	*Pupil-teacher ratio* (H) (Average weight—3.42 %)
Category frequency count	G—3 H—2 M—0 R&D—1	G—4 H—2 M—1 R&D—1	G—1 H—2 M—2 R&D—2	G—3 H—3 M—2 R&D—2	G—2 H—1 M—2 R&D—1	G—2 H—3 M—2 R&D—1	G—4 H—1 M—2 R&D—1	G—2 H—4 M—2 R&D—1

Remarks G & G–C government related issues including capital availability represented by G–C (total 21 counts including 6 counts of capital availability), *H* human capital issues (18 counts), *M* market capital issues (13 counts), *R&D* research and development (10 counts)

average explaining power of each enhancing/impeding factor before and after the turning point

the explaining power of Israeli enhancing factors after the 2008 turning point is the strongest (28.21 %).

In Fig. 3.31, Jordan's turning points are 2007 and 2009. The four rectangular 3D graphs on the left hand side indicate that except market capital at the middle capability region, the other three capitals are positioned at the low capability region (20 % below average). Table 3.3 shows that government related (G) and human capital related (H) issues constitute a majority of impeding factors (6 out of 10 counts). "Corporate tax encouragement", "convenience of establishing new firms" and "capital availability" are government related issues. In addition, "public expenditure on education" and "R&D % of GDP" are impeding factors both before and after the turning point, indicating the lasting problems. "Capital availability" as an impeding factor agrees with the explanation in Chap. 2 that Jordan relies on external grants to support its economy. However, the explaining weight of Jordan's impeding factors (5.30 and 4.29 %) is weaker than its enhancing factors (15.48 and 15.13 %) both before and after the turning point.

Based on Fig. 3.32, South Africa's turning point is 2007. The four rectangular 3D graphs on the left hand side of the figure indicate that all four types of capital are in the low capability region (20 % below average). Table 3.3 shows that the first two impeding factors before the turning point are government related (G) "capital availability" and "transparency of government policy". Although human capital related (H) issue has three counts, "skilled labor" before the turning point was the fifth factor and "employee training" and "public expenditure on education" are the third and fourth impeding factors after the turning point with a light weight of 4.16 % only. A good sign is that "capital availability" being the first impeding factor before the turning point has turned to the first enhancing factor after the turning point. This finding somewhat explains South Africa's good recovery after the financial crisis. However, its other impeding factors before the turning point (average weight 22.91 %), such as "image of country" and "openness to culture" deserve some attention.

Figure 3.33 shows 2009 is Turkey's turning point. The four rectangular 3D graphs on the left hand side of the figure indicate that except market capital in the middle capability region, the other three capitals are positioned at the low capability region (20 % below average). Table 3.3 shows that government (G) related issues are the major enhancing factors, including "government efficiency" both before and after the turning point, as well as "corporate tax encouragement" and "capital availability" after the turning point. The explaining power of enhancing factors is higher after than before the turning point (18.40 vs. 7.61 %). Human capital (H) related issues that impeded its GDP growth included "public expenditure on education", "higher education enrollment" and "pupil-teacher ratio". Its impeding factors of "openness to culture" and "export of goods" also deserved some attention.

To summarize Table 3.3 for an overall suggestion, we count the frequency of both enhancing and impeding factors by categories, please refer to the last row of the table. Government related issue (G & G–C) has a total of 21 counts. Since capital availability is a concern during the financial crisis, we particularly highlight it by G–C. Out of the 21 counts, six counts are capital availability with two each for Israel and South Africa, and one each for Jordan (impeding factor) and Turkey (enhancing factor). For Israel and South Africa, the capital availability problem before the turning point has become enhancing factor after the turning point. Among the 21 counts of government related issues, 11 of them are impeding factors and 10 of them are enhancing factors. Human capital (H) related issues have 18 counts and 12 of them are impeding factors. Market capital (M)-related issues have 13 counts and 7 of them are impeding factors. R&D related issues have 10 counts and 5 of them are impeding factors. In this country cluster, human capital related issues turn out to be a focal area that deserves special attention, especially for Jordan, South Africa, and Turkey.

For the average weight, enhancing factors after the turning point have a stronger explaining power in Israel (28.21 %), Jordan (15.13 %), South Africa (21.92 %), and Turkey (18.40 %) than before the turning point. On the contrary, impeding factors before the turning point have a stronger explaining power in Jordan (5.30 %), South Africa (22.91 %), and Turkey (7.30 %) than after the turning point.

Figure 3.34 identifies the efficiency drivers (positive term) for each individual country. Efficiency targeting is akin to benchmarking. Efficiency represents GDP in this 3D software program. Since the U.S. has both good NIC and GDP, it serves as a good benchmarking target for these four countries. In Fig. 3.34, the stacked small horizontal stripes are the deficiency factors of each country benchmarking the GDP of the U.S. in 2010. The length of the stripes represents the degree of deficiency. For easier comparison, we list the first five deficiency factors of each country in Table 3.4.

The results indicate that Israel needs to strengthen, in sequence, its "patents", "R&D researchers", "IP rights protection", "computers in use per capita" and "image of country". Jordan needs to strength its "computers in use per capita", "patents", "basic research", "enterprise-university cooperation" and "business R&D". South Africa needs to strengthen its "computers in use per capita", "patents", "internet subscribers", "skilled labor" and "business R&D". Turkey needs to strengthen its "computers in use per capita", "patents", "business R&D", "internet subscribers" and "basic research".

With the USA as the benchmark country, irrespective to the sequence of deficiency, the common areas that these four countries need to improve include patents (four counts), computers in use per capita (four counts), business R&D (three counts), basic research (two counts), and internet subscribers (two counts). That is, areas that require further enhancement are quite similar for these four countries. Among the above five common indicators, three (patents, business R&D, and basic research) facilitate the accumulation of renewal capital. Chapter 3 explains that renewal capital explains more GDP growth, particularly for emerging economies. This finding points out a clear direction for Jordan, South Africa, and Turkey to strategize their national development.

Based on the average deficiency (negative term) percentage reported in Table 3.4 and Fig. 3.34, South Africa has the most amount of work in order to

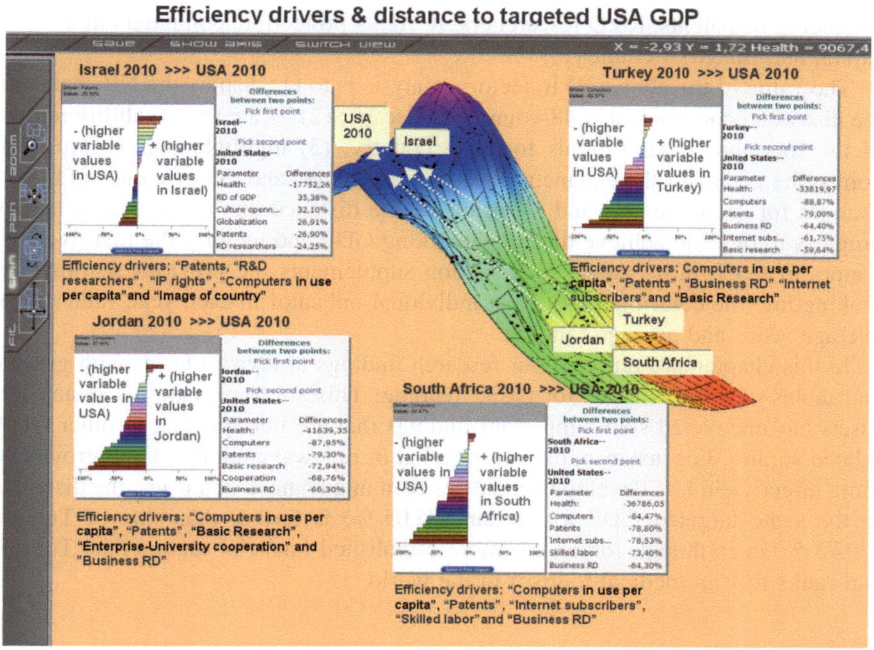

Fig. 3.34 Efficiency drivers and distance to targeted GDP of the U.S

Table 3.4 The first five efficiency drivers targeting GDP of the U.S

Efficiency driver	Israel	Jordan	South Africa	Turkey
Factor #1	Patents	Computers in use per capita	Computers in use per capita	Computer in use per capita
Factor #2	R&D researchers	Patents	Patents	Patents
Factor #3	IP rights protection	Basic research	Internet subscribers	Business R&D
Factor #4	computers in use per capita	Enterprise-university cooperation	Skilled labor	Internet subscribers
Factor #5	Image of country	Business R&D	Business R&D	Basic research
Average deficiency percentage of the above five drivers	21.26 %	75.05 %	75.90 %	70.73 %

achieve the target GDP (U.S.), followed by Jordan, Turkey, and Israel. In other words, Israel will have the shortest route to reach the preset GDP goal through enhancing its patents, R&D researchers, IP rights protection, computers in use per capita, and image of country.

The value of the above 3D trajectory analysis is to (1) display the NIC paths of the discussed countries on a 48-country landscape; (2) locate the capability region of the four individual capitals for each country; (3) highlight the NIC turning points, the details of the enhancing or impeding factor, and the dynamics of factor changes for each country; and (4) calculate the distance that each country has to progress in order to achieve the benchmarking GDP and identify the first five key factors to reach those goals. This section supplements the previous sections by looking into the contribution of each individual indicator in each year, rather than average score and average ranking.

In this chapter, we reported our research findings in layman terms with graphs and tables of various types for easier reading. This study on national intangible assets has uncovered some important findings that are not apparent in other GDP related studies. For instance, the contribution of renewal capital to GDP growth is more effective in less developed countries than in advanced countries; the distance to the same targeted GDP for Jordan (75.05 %) is farther than that of Turkey (70.73 %) even though Jordan has more established financial sectors than Turkey and ranks fifth in medical tourism in the world.

Chapter 4
Beyond the 2008 Global Financial Crisis

This chapter reports activities after 2010, a time regarded as the aftermath of the 2008 global financial crisis, which was formally announced at the end of 2009 (Kehoe 2010; OECD 2010). Although many European countries slipped back into another recession due to sovereign debt problems at the end of 2010, we use 2010 as a dividing line in order to be consistent with the reports of non-EU country clusters in this booklet series. The four countries reported in this volume have recovered from the financial crisis in varying degrees.

After the 2008 global recession, factors that caused it have become known. A lack of financial system supervision and oversight is a key reason. Although the guideline of maintaining a government deficit of no more than 3 % and public debt not to exceed 60 % of the GDP has been globally known for more than a decade, many countries were not aware of its importance until this financial crisis. In this volume, Israel and Jordan had government debt over 90 and 80 % of their GDP in 2005, respectively. Despite Israel's fast recovery from the crisis, its scope of impact was much more serious than its 2001 dot.com bubble burst. However, these two countries have been able to reduce their debt level significantly (to 77.3 and 58.7 % in 2010) after the financial crisis as shown in Fig. 2.2.

In what follows, in the sequence of Israel, Jordan, South Africa, and Turkey, we briefly describe what happened in each individual country after 2010.

Israel

In 2010, the Israeli economy moved back quickly into a growth trend with about 4.5 % growth (Brosh 2011). Its financial market has achieved a sharp recovery since early 2009, offsetting most of the losses triggered by the global financial crisis in 2008 (Economic Freedom 2012). Israeli real GDP growth was 4.7 % in 2011 and 2.7 % in 2012 (Global Finance 2012) due to the expected slowdown of growth in world trade and erosion in the competitiveness of Israeli exports (Brosh 2011).

C. Y.-Y. Lin et al., *National Intellectual Capital and the Financial Crisis in Israel, Jordan, South Africa, and Turkey*, SpringerBriefs in Economics,
DOI: 10.1007/978-1-4614-7981-9_4, © The Author(s) 2014

Israel's ability to ride out the global recession relatively well was principally due to its past growth, Fiscal and Monetary Policy, and regulation regime (Rosenberg 2010). Israel achieved around 5.2 % growth between 2004 and 2007. It also exploited the years of strong growth to reduce debt to a little over 70 % of the GDP in 2008 from 99.8 % in 2003 and the budget deficit fell to 0.02 % of the GDP in 2007 from 5.3 % in 2003 (Rosenberg 2010). During Israeli policy thrust toward deregulation, banking and property sectors remain heavily regulated. In other words, Israel had a good economic stance prior to this financial crisis.

Several other reasons also protected Israel from severe external financial impact. They include the absence of a real-estate bubble, relatively low household debts, relatively high rate of private savings (an effective "safety cushion" during extreme crisis conditions), banks relying more on deposits for capital than wholesale funds, high concentration of value-added high-tech products, and lessons learned from the dot.com era (Brosh 2011; Buchwald 2009; Rosenberg 2010). In addition, throughout the crisis, manufacturers implemented flexible methods of employment, such as reducing overtime, collective vacations, and shortening the working week, which enabled them to avoid widespread dismissals, and retain skilled workers for "the day after" (Brosh 2011). Productive cooperation between the representatives of the employers (Federation of Israeli Economic Organizations), the workers (Histadrut trade union), and government (Brosh 2011) was also an effective arrangement that enabled them to work through the crisis collaboratively.

With the above stated status, the OECD estimated that the total cost of Israeli stimulus measures to 2010, including the cost of tax increases, was no more than 0.5 % of its GDP (Rosenberg 2010). In fact, the Israeli government adopted some measures antithetical to a stimulus, raising the value-added and other taxes and increasing employers' National Insurance Institute contributions (Rosenberg 2010). Despite the Israeli government having offered guarantees to help commercial banks raise capital, it turned out that the banks had no need of the assistance. As of January 2010, only about 10 % of government supported funds to buy corporate bonds had been used. Likewise, only about one-fourth of the fund for small and medium-sized business had been taken up (Rosenberg 2010). The Bank of Israel began raising interest rates in the summer of 2009 when the economy began to show signs of recovery (CIA 2012).

Nevertheless, the Israeli economy remains prone to risk due to the prospects for a slow recovery in developed economies. Although Israel is redirecting more of its exports to the stronger economies of Asia, the transition takes some time (Rosenberg 2010).

Jordan

After the financial crisis, Jordan was still facing weak growth and high unemployment, especially among youth, even though Jordan had a GDP growth of 2.5 % in 2011, the same as what the IMF estimated (Barakat et al. 2012; Global

Finance 2012). As an oil and food import-dependent country, Jordan has developed a widening trade deficit due to its rising import bill (Ali 2011; CIA 2012). As a result, the kingdom had to solicit an exceptional amount in foreign grants to cover additional spending earmarked for its social safety net (Barakat et al. 2012). Gulf cooperation council (GCC) states had provided critical financial support to Jordan's economy in 2011, including grants of US$1.4 billion (5.2 % of GDP) from Saudi Arabia (Ali 2011). Its public finances also came under pressure in 2011, because of the increased commodity subsidies and other social spending aimed at quelling domestic disturbances (Barakat et al. 2012). In addition, its domestic sluggishness comes within the context of the arising regional political turmoil, the increased domestic uncertainty, and the weakening global economy (Barakat et al. 2012). King Abdullah has already reshuffled the cabinet three times since November 2010 (Ali 2011); however, Jordan's total recovery remains uncertain.

At the level of external accounts, rising commodity prices and declining foreign receipts were contributing to a worsening current account balance despite increasing exports (Barakat et al. 2012). In 2011, Jordan's central bank reserves decreased to US$11 billion from US$12.3 billion a year before, public debt increased to US$19 billion (67.4 % of GDP) from US$17.7 billion in 2010, with the fiscal deficit reaching 6.2 % of the GDP, and the FDI into Jordan fell by 17.7 % relative to the corresponding period of 2010 on the back of regional political concerns (Ali 2011; Barakat et al. 2012; Global Finance 2012). In addition, stock prices reported an additional decline of 12.6 % in 2011 and tourist arrivals also declined sharply in 2011 by 22 % year to year, widening the current account deficit (Ali 2011; Barakat et al. 2012). Higher government wages and salaries and higher subsidies further widened the deficit (excluding grants) to US$1.7 billion (5.9 % of GDP) in the first nine months of 2011 (Ali 2011).

The 2012 outlook for Jordan is also challenging (Ali 2011). The IMF was expecting an extension of the low growth trend for yet another year with real GDP growth forecasted at 2.75 % for 2012, as high commodity import prices, rising sovereign financing costs and regional socio-political unrest are apt to adversely affect the Jordanian economy (Barakat et al. 2012). The 2012 deficit is likely to widen further to 7.5 % of the GDP. Therefore, funding the deficit will be the main challenge (Ali 2011).

On the positive side, the Jordanian dinar (JOD) pegged to the US dollar is an important pillar of financial stability (Ali 2011). The Central Bank of Jordan also adopted the international best practices (Basel II) to enhance the soundness of the banking institutions and strengthen their capacity in the area of risk management (Al-Mahrouq 2009).

South Africa

Compared with other developing countries, South Africa's economy has done relatively well (Baxter 2012). After the financial crisis, growth in Africa accelerated to 2.8 % in 2010 and rose to 3.5 % in 2011 (Global Finance 2012; Gurria 2010). With external conditions becoming more favorable, housing prices picked up and leading indicators signaled growing strength. Furthermore, the economy is being boosted by the staging of the 2010 World Cup (Gurria 2010).

A major factor of South Africa's resilience to this global financial crisis is its free floating of the exchange rate, which allowed the Rand (South African currency) to follow its function as an adjustment parameter (Draper et al. 2009). In the past, South Africa has not been directly hit by any of the famous global financial crises, mainly because of its prudent regulatory steps (Dlamini 2010; Draper et al. 2009). A very strong regulatory framework for the financial system, which is supported by strong regulatory institutions, has cushioned South Africa from the negative effects of the recent crisis (Dlamini 2010). In the period preceding the financial crisis, South Africa's banking system also remained stable, and banks were adequately capitalized. The South African banking sector's capital-adequacy ratio remained above the minimum requirement of 9.5 % and reached 13.0 % at the end of December 2008 (Dlamini 2010). The minimal integration of the South African financial system into the world financial market also minimized its exposure to the riskiest financial products. Another key factor contributing to South Africa's resilience is its well-praised social partners system. The social partners consisted of representatives drawn from the labor, business, government, and social communities, who were also responsible for guiding national development and policy implementation (Dlamini 2010).

During the financial crisis, the national industrial policy framework (NIPF) began to promote diversification of the South African economy, particularly through building manufacturing industry and growing associated exports in order to sustain the current account deficit and address its unemployment crisis (Draper et al. 2009). Also, during the financial crisis despite increased lobbying from individual labor and business organizations, South African government refused to issue bailout packages, preferring instead to make long-term interventions focused on growth and development (Dlamini 2010). However, its fiscal stimulus includes significant levels of public investment in infrastructure till 2012 has been made available in the national budget. This investment will be used to expand and improve road and rail networks, public transport and port operations, dams, water and sanitation infrastructure, housing construction, information and communications technology, energy-generation capacity, and education and health infrastructure (Dlamini 2010). These measures have laid a firmer foundation for South Africa's economic development.

En route to national recovery, the government also realized that a growing vibrant private sector is the basis for creating and retaining employment in the South African economy (Baxter 2012). However, the decline of South African

Business Confidence Index highlights an unstable and weakening business environment (Baxter 2012; Mail and Guardian 2012). To attract foreign capital, and to promote business and consumer confidence, South Africa needs to have stable and predictable economic policies (Baxter 2012).

Turkey

After the financial crisis, Turkey's macroeconomic stability was well maintained, and stimulus measures, which included temporary cuts in indirect taxes, have been largely phased out (Heritage 2012). Decline in the business investment has slowed down (Babacan 2009). A major driver of this relative improvement was the recovery in the household private consumption which parallels the rise in the household confidence (Babacan 2009).

In addition, Turkey's well-regulated financial markets and banking system helped weather the global financial crisis, thus the GDP rebounded strongly in 2010, as exports returned to normal levels (CIA 2012). Turkish banks had not engaged in substantial trading in derivative instruments of the kind that created problems in industrial countries; the banks were largely satisfied with the relatively high yields they received on Turkish government bonds (Togan 2010). In addition, bank deposits are the primary investment instrument for most Turkish citizens, therefore individual investors had very limited equity market exposure either directly or through mutual funds, nor do they have any exposure to corporate bonds or derivative instruments (Togan 2010). Furthermore, since housing prices have not fallen substantially, Turkish consumers have not faced any significant wealth destruction (Togan 2010). The stock value of FDI stood at US$174 billion at year-end in 2010; however, inflows have slowed considerably in light of continuing economic turmoil in Europe, the source of much of Turkey's FDI (CIA 2012).

In January 2010, international credit rating agency Moody's upgraded Turkey's government bond rating from Ba3 to Ba2 (Turkish Press 2010). World Bank said that Turkey's economy had taken on a recovery track from a global economic recession and European Commission also reported that Turkey would be the fastest growing economy in Europe (Turkish Press 2010). In November 2010, Fitch Ratings affirmed Turkey's Credit Rating as BB(+) and revised its credit outlook to "Positive." Turkish car market grew 30.8 % year-on-year between January and November 2010. In December 2010, the International Monetary Fund voiced an optimistic outlook on Turkish economy and predicted that its output would surpass its pre-crisis level by a comfortable margin, one of the few countries in Europe to achieve this milestone (Turkish Press 2010). In 2011, Turkey achieved a GDP growth of 8.5 % (Global Finance 2012).

Specifically, the rating agencies' favorable comments on Turkey include the following. Turkey's floating exchange rate and inflation targeting regime are strong points during and after the financial crisis. Debt tolerance is enhanced by strong banking sector, relatively deep local markets, strong debt management capacities, and good debt service record. Turkish economy's ability to rebound from external shocks represents that it has passed the "stress test" of its policy reforms and policy credibility over the last decade (Gonene et al. 2010). Turkey's local capital markets are continuing to develop, enabling the government to lengthen maturities of local currency debt (Gonene et al. 2010). Furthermore, the industry used the financial crisis to expand into new export markets and to reduce its dependence on EU markets (Gonene et al. 2010). Apparently, it is a successful diversification strategy.

In spite of these promising signs, Turkish economy continues to be burdened by a high current account deficit and remains dependent on often volatile, short-term investment to finance its trade deficit (CIA 2012). In addition, Turkey's relatively high policy uncertainty and fiscal imbalances leave the economy vulnerable to destabilizing shifts in investor confidence (CIA 2012). The rating agencies also suggested the government for more fiscal transparency, complying with international standard general government data, and reporting for strengthening its administrative infrastructure (Gonene et al. 2010). Furthermore, political risk weighs on Turkey's rating. The country is ranked in the bottom 21st percentile in the World Bank's political stability index.

Chapter 5
Future Perspective and Policy Implications

By late 2012, more than 4 years have passed since the outbreak of 2008 global financial crisis. It is time to reflect upon what happened during the past few years and what can be learned from this crisis experience for preventive actions in the future.

In January 2012, the International Monetary Fund announced that global recovery was threatened by intensifying strains in the Euro area; thus financial conditions have deteriorated, growth prospects have dimmed, and downside risks have escalated (IMF 2012). The Euro area economy went into a mild recession in 2012. The effects of bank deleveraging on the real economy may surface again and the impact of additional fiscal consolidation may heighten. Even growth in developing economies that had traditionally remained resilient was expected to slow down because of the worsening external environment and a weakening of internal demand (IMF 2012).

The global investment prospects continue to be clouded by the significant uncertainties with the sliding economy.

However, situations of the countries reported in this volume are steadily progressing, except Jordan. No matter whether a particular country experienced fast or slow recovery, lessons can be learned by going through the process of planning and implementing stimulus package and continuing the national reform for sustainability in the future. In other words, the economic crisis provides an ideal opportunity to examine the soundness of a nation's economic system and the effectiveness of national governance.

In this chapter, we first present the prospects of these four countries, and then describe their potential challenges in the future. What we have described hereunder is mainly based upon the OECD economic survey report whenever available, supplementing by other relevant reports. The prospects and challenges are meant to provide points of thought for discussion and do not represent an exhaustive list. This chapter finishes with some policy implications.

C. Y.-Y. Lin et al., *National Intellectual Capital and the Financial Crisis in Israel, Jordan, South Africa, and Turkey*, SpringerBriefs in Economics,
DOI: 10.1007/978-1-4614-7981-9_5,

Prospects

Although these four countries have not totally recovered from the 2008 global financial crisis, there are already signs of promising prospects, which are briefly explained hereunder.

Israel

Although hit hard by the 2008 global financial crisis, Israel recovered relatively well for a combination of factors. They include massive investment in R&D, a high level of flexibility, innovation and creativity, openness to trade with countries around the world, controlled governance, responsible monetary and fiscal policy, and cooperation between representatives of the employers and the employees (Brosh 2011). The main drivers for Israel's further development can be described from the perspectives of economic system, financial system, technology, workforce, and the discovery of a natural gas field.

Economic System

The Israeli economic system has the following features, which may facilitate its future development:

1. Free-market reforms and a reduction in public spending stimulated Israeli growth (Buchwald 2009). For example, total government expenditures fell to 42.9 % of GDP; in addition, its privatization has accelerated (Economic Freedom 2012).
2. Investors demonstrate confidence investing in Israel's economy. FDI Foreign investors see their investment in Israel as long-term profitable assets and continue to express their confidence in the Israeli economy. This trust is shown by the establishment of research and development centers, the founding of manufacturing plants, mergers and acquisitions, and other types of collaboration (Buchwald 2009; State of Israel 2012).
3. Flexibility that adapts quickly to changing conditions is a success factor. Israeli exporters successfully divert exports of goods to Asia from the troubled EU area during this financial crisis. As a result, trade to Asia rose from 15 % in 2007 to about 20 % in 2010, while the share of the European Union decreased to 30 % (Brosh 2011).
4. Israel is open to global trade with investment encouragement and talent retention measures (Brosh 2011; Economic Freedom 2012; Swirski 2010). Israeli government aggressively signs free trade agreements, thus about 65 % of its foreign trade was derived from countries with the free trade agreements. In addition, corporate tax will be gradually decreased from 24 % in 2011 to

18 % in 2016 to attract foreign and domestic investors. Also, cuts in the income tax were openly promoted as a way of giving the entrepreneurial and managerial class a reason to stay in Israel—rather than emigrate to the higher incomes and a more secure environment, such as Silicon Valley.
5. Israeli government increased its supporting capability to domestic consumer demand with public assets portfolio reached a high level of about 26 % in 2010, above its level prior to the crisis (Brosh 2011).

Financial System

Israeli financial system played a key role withholding the economy from seriously impacted by this financial crisis and would continue to support Israel's future development with the following features (Buchwald 2009; Economic Freedom 2012; State of Israel 2012):

1. Israel has few complex financial instruments in the capital markets and was insulated from the U.S. subprime real estate market.
2. Israel has high and rising foreign exchange reserves with surplus in the current account of the balance of payments.
3. Israel has a strong banking system and its strict fiscal policy serves as a robust buffer against foreign financial pressures and ensures the economy's quick recovery.
4. Israeli government continuously works on public debt and deficit reduction, which facilitates the building of a more resilient financial system. For example, it has reduced public debt from 100 % of GDP in 2003 to around 80 % in 2007 and 74.3 % in 2011.

Technology

Israel's reputation as a leader of technological innovation is well-established internationally and continues to gain ground for future development. Its features include (Rosenberg 2010; State of Israel 2012):

1. Israel's high-technology industry is unusual by world standards because of its focus on start-up companies and on research and development. As a result, foreigner investors' confidence in Israel is strong. Multinational corporations have been active in Israel for decades and their motivation to invest in the local economy has been unshaken by security issues and the financial crisis.
2. Israel counts 140 scientists and technicians and 135 engineers for every 10,000 people, the highest ratio in the world. It spends more on R&D than its developed-country peers—about 4.7 % of GDP in 2007, compared with 3.0–3.6 % for the next three biggest-spending economies.

3. Israeli researchers are developing technology with commercial applications, as evidenced by the number of utility patents per million. Israel ranks fourth in the world on a per capita basis, behind only Taiwan, Japan, and the United States.
4. Israel's water and clean-tech technologies sectors have become recognized worldwide due to the country's first-hand, proven knowledge in these fields and the global increase in demand for efficient water and clean energy technologies.

Workforce

Israel's greatest natural resource is its skilled workforce—highly motivated, resourceful, and independent—they enable Israel to stay ahead of the competition (Brosh 2011; State of Israel 2012) with the following features:

1. Israel's workforce is particularly competitive because of the informal but effective get-down-to-business culture, exceptional ingenuity, and entrepreneurial spirit. The combination of culture, skill, and initiative creates a flexible, working system that allows for great adaptability while producing breakthrough technologies and quick time-to-market solutions.
2. Israel has the world's highest level of technological intensity. With massive investments in R&D and a high-quality skilled work force, the Israeli economy has become innovative and sophisticated, rapidly adapting itself to the changing requirements of international markets.
3. The continuing decline in the unemployment rate after the financial crisis and the real increase in average wages will support growth of domestic demand in the future.
4. Israel has established a good social partnership between the representatives of the employers in the business sector and employees through the trade union which enables Israel to resolve labor disputes and reduce the number of strikes and lockouts in the economy.

The Discovery of a Natural Gas Field

In the future, the Israeli economy is expected to benefit from the great discovery of a natural gas near the coast of Israel. According to estimates, there is a quantity of natural gas amounting to about 80–90 billion dollars. Such a discovery will change the face of the business environment in Israel, with significant decreases in energy costs to the economy. Furthermore, massive investment will be required to set up infrastructures to transport and distribute the natural gas, which by itself will be an additional growth engine for the various business sectors (Brosh 2011).

Jordan

Although Jordan was not doing well after the financial crisis, it still has good features that may help the country develop in the future. They include its economic system, financial system, fiscal reform, educational reform, workforce, and medical tourism.

Economic System

1. Jordanian manufacturers have a good reputation, especially in the region with well-established contacts and trade links.
2. Jordan has the most open and most competitive market in the region, with no restrictions on foreign ownership and free repatriation of profits (Al-Mahrouq 2009).
3. There is a growing interest in Business Processes Outsourcing in Jordan, especially call-centers (Al-Mahrouq 2009).
4. Jordan acceded to the World Trade Organization in 2000, and began to participate in the European Free Trade Association in 2001 (CIA 2012), which has opened many opportunities for Jordan.
5. The 2009 AT Kearney Global Services Location Index ranked Jordan 9th out of 50 countries in providing global services. Jordan made it into the top ten mainly because of its solid information technology capabilities, favorable business environment, and a well-educated work force (Al-Mahrouq 2009).

Financial System

1. The competitive position of Jordan's banking sector has been strong since 1925, due to a solid internationally based legal framework, good human resources, and good information technology quality with a proactive regulatory supervision (Al-Mahrouq 2009).
2. During the financial crisis, banks in Jordan ran their business in accordance with a conservative approach toward liquidity risks and have proven liquidity diligence.
3. Jordan did not use complex financial instruments and was not exposed to the problem assets. As a result, Arab investors find the Jordanian market, despite its small size, more durable, and less prone to fluctuations, thus have increased their investment in Jordan (Alnajjar et al. 2011).
4. Jordanian banking sector's capital adequacy ratio reached 18.2 % in June 2011, which was way above minimum requirements and compared favorably to regional and global benchmarks (Barakat et al. 2012).

5. Jordan was an aggressive initiator to call for the cooperation of financial institutions in the region in order to respond better to future external shocks (Al-Mahrouq 2009).

Fiscal Reform

After the financial crisis, there was a USAID supported fiscal reform project to help the Jordanian government achievement the following objectives (Jaradat 2010). Successful implementation of these programs will greatly strengthen Jordanian fiscal system.

1. Improve efficiency of use of public resources through stronger public financial management.
2. Establish a result-oriented government.
3. Enhance revenue mobilization through better revenue administration.
4. Adopt resource-saving reforms in selected government programs through sound policy analysis initiated from the Ministry of Finance.
5. Increase efficiency in trading across borders.

Educational Reform

Jordan implemented an ambitious and comprehensive program for education reform called education reform for knowledge economy (ERfKE) (Warlop and Sayed 2009). This program is currently regarded as a model for educational reform throughout the Arab region. The transition rate to higher education has ranged between 79 and 85 % of secondary school graduates over the past 5 years. During the process, Jordan also ensures a high level of gender parity.

Workforce

1. Jordan's competitiveness is founded on its human capital. For many years, Jordan has been a seedbed for skilled and experienced professionals in the Middle East.
2. Highly qualified specialists and factory workforce are the sector's assets in Jordan. For example, the pharmaceutical industry employs many PhD's, as the production requires complicated formulas combined with a high extent of research and development (Al-Mahrouq 2009).

Medical Tourism

Medical tourism sector is thought to be one of the main contributors to Jordan's economy. It brings revenue of around one billion U.S. dollars annually and displays a steady increase of about 10 % of foreign patients per annum. World Bank medical tourism experts ranked Jordan as top country in the Arab region and 5th in the world as a medical tourism hub (Al-Mahrouq 2009).

South Africa

The South African economy benefits from relatively good levels of trade freedom, business freedom, and financial freedom (Heritage 2012). South Africa is the economic hub of Sub-Saharan Africa and one of the world's largest producers and exporters of gold and platinum. Mining, services, manufacturing, and agriculture rival similar sectors in the developed world (Heritage 2012). Future prospects of South Africa can be elaborated from its economic system, financial system, green products, and social partners system.

Economic System

1. South Africa's regulatory environment encourages competitiveness and flexibility.
2. During the financial crisis, capital flight rush from emerging economies (Heritage 2012). Simultaneous to the outflow of these funds, in 2008 South Africa also had the highest inflows of FDI over the last 5 years. Apparently, investors still see the macroeconomic conditions in South Africa as favorable to justify a long-term engagement (Draper et al. 2009).
3. In South Africa, private investment outpaces public investment or consumption, indicating the confidence of private investors which energizing the economy.
4. South Africa has managed the transition period after the end of Apartheid rather well and has good chances to further improve the governance structure. Besides macroeconomic policy and institutions, microeconomic policies such as competition policy, labor market regulation, regulation in general, and trade policy all facilitate its future national development.
5. South Africa benefited a lot from the net capital inflows, which can be used to invest further for creating new jobs, lifting the living standard of the poorest and increasing saving in the country.

Financial System

1. Monetary stability is relatively good in South Africa with the government still influencing prices through regulation, state-owned enterprises, and other support programs (Draper et al. 2009; Heritage 2012).
2. Despite the South African economy having been hard hit by the global financial crisis, no exchange rate shock or "sudden stop" has been experienced. This explains its relatively sound financial system.

Green Products

In South Africa, there has been a fresh interest in green jobs, the design and implementation of green buildings, and the development of a payment for ecosystem goods and services. An example is payment for the green energy generated by the rural poor (Blignaut 2009).

Social Partners System

In South Africa, there is a special social partners (government, labor, business, and community collaboration) system. The framework has been praised at the international level for bringing together social partners in forging a common response. During the financial crisis, it functioned very well in a sustainable manner.

In 1994, the South African government put this structure in place which assures that social dialogue accompanies the development of economic policies and that civil society has both an opportunity and a platform to articulate its voice in this process (Dlamini 2010). From a government perspective, once a relevant government department has a specific economic policy, it must submit it to the National Economic Development and Labor Council (NEDLAC), whose stakeholders (drawn from government, labor, business, and community groups) then debate and come to an agreement on particular policy measures. These measures are then introduced in the form of a bill for debate within parliament, which must also make room for public participation in its structures and processes before the bill becomes law.

Turkey

Turkey's political stability, structural reforms, coupled with the prudent fiscal and monetary policy have paved the way for uninterrupted growth periods of 27 quarters up to the last quarter of 2008 (Babacan 2009). Its prospect may be described from the perspective of economic system, its Medium Term Program, and innovation.

Economic System

1. Turkey's business environment has gradually become more streamlined and efficient as a bridge between East and West (Heritage 2012).
2. Its private sector is growing, though the state remains heavily involved in the economy.
3. Turkey's GDP and GDP per capita almost tripled in 2008, comparing that in 2002. This astounding economic performance has placed Turkey as the second fastest growing economy among the OECD members and now Turkey is the 17th largest economy in the world (Babacan 2009).
4. Turkey has emerged as a top investment destination due to the elimination of bureaucratic barriers to a large extent, improvement in tax system, facilitation of profit transfers, and successful privatization programs.
5. Foreign direct investment inflows which were US$1.1 billion on average between 1993 and 2002, increased gradually afterwards and reached to US$20.1 billion on average between 2006 and 2008 (Babacan 2009).
6. A shift from labor intensive product exports toward relatively technology intensive exports have contributed to Turkey's recent remarkable achievement (Babacan 2009). Total exports which were US$36.1 billion in 2002 reached US$132 billion in 2008.
7. Turkish entrepreneurs' ambition in widening and strengthening their trade links with the rest of the world and their success in differentiating their products and services yielded more than a fourfold increase in the export volume between 2002 and 2008 mentioned above (Togan 2010).

Medium Term Program

Turkish Medium Term Program announced in September 2009 outlined the country's fiscal targets covering 2010–2012 period (Babacan 2009; Togan 2010). The main purposes of the program are to establish a framework that enables Turkey to achieve a sustainable growth rate after the financial crisis and to increase society's welfare. On the fiscal front, the government expects gradual improvement, such as deficit reduces to 3.2 % by 2012. Structural reforms are to increase competitiveness and flexibility of the economy through converging the growth rate gradually to creating jobs, reducing the inflation rate, and improving the public sector balances.

Innovation

To improve innovative capacity, Turkish government introduced a new and comprehensive Research and Development Law in 2008. With this law, the government aimed to accelerate both foreign and local R&D investment and develop an environment more conducive to innovation. Government authorities in

Turkey are also moving toward enhancing the socioeconomic impact of cultural life, with the awareness of its importance. Based on Creative Economy Report, Istanbul has been selected as the Cultural Capital of Europe in 2010. A series of arts events, cultural festivals, and an important symposium have been taking place that year. In addition, Turkey has the potential to serve as the intersection of the West and East in innovation.

Challenges

Although governments of these four countries have exerted their best efforts to weather this financial crisis and most of them have returned to or even surpassed its precrisis path. However, many challenges remain to be tackled. This section briefly introduces the issues that need special attention for each country.

Israel

Although Israel turned to be stronger after the financial crisis, there are still challenges lying ahead, including security concern, constraints of current technology sector, human capital and education issues, overseas production, and social inequality.

Security Concern

Israel's geopolitical uncertainty—the threats of fighting on Israel's Gaza and Lebanon borders and Iran's nuclear program—is a great threat to its future development. The regional political instability may deter customers, partners, and investors. These risks are magnified by Israel's history of weak and divided governments (Rosenberg 2010).

Constraints of Current Technology Sector

Israel is a small economy with a limited labor supply and is distant from key markets. Its technology sector is relatively disconnected from broader domestic economic policy, little concerned with local demand, financial markets, or regulatory issues (Rosenberg 2010). Over the past two decades, the sector has developed into an industry with a recurrent cycle of start-up companies that conceive and develop new technology, finance it with venture capital, and prove it in the marketplace before selling themselves to bigger overseas companies. This process is now being duplicated by its emergent biotechnology and clean technologies sectors (Rosenberg 2010). The challenge for Israel is how to expand and deepen its knowledge-based industries to narrow the social and economic imbalances, rather than over reliance on high-technology start-up companies.

In addition, if the Israeli start-up continues to exist as a separate entity to serve in R&D roles, Israelis do not get the opportunity to develop the skills in marketing, finance, and managing a large organization. So long as Israel's knowledge economy is concentrated narrowly on technology start-ups, the country will continue to face problems of high unemployment, poverty, and income inequality (Rosenberg 2010). Although the start-up industry is an asset to Israel, more start-up companies should be encouraged to mature into sustainable business enterprises.

Human Capital and Education Issues

Israel needs to ensure that it can continue to produce good quality and enough quantity of people that enables the technology industry to grow and develop. In addition, it is also important that the institutional structures can foster the development of other knowledge-intensive industries, including design, medical services, education, and media/entertainment by creating more jobs (Rosenberg 2010).

Regarding Israel's future generation, students perform poorly by international standards in primary and secondary education. In addition, classroom sizes are above average even though Israeli education spending is close to the OECD average on a per capita basis (Rosenberg 2010). Teacher pay is low relative to other developed countries, which will not attract talented people to educate the rising generation. The quality of Israeli higher education has also deteriorated, although the number of degrees awarded has grown (Rosenberg 2010).

Overseas Production

Over the years, the trend of shifting production lines and development activities from Israel to overseas accelerated. This trend threatens the future of the domestic Israeli industry. According to a survey carried out by the Economic Research Department in February 2010, around 2013, 45 % of industrial plants would have manufacturing activity overseas (Brosh 2011). Such trend will further reduce the job opportunities in Israel.

Social Inequality

The gap between the rich and the poor in Israel is the highest in OECD (Elman 2011). Israel's poverty rate of about 21 % was highest among all OECD countries in 2005. In addition, income inequality in Israel was among the highest in the OECD, with only the United States, Portugal, Turkey, and Mexico exceeding it. As noted earlier, Israel's unemployment rate has remained high even during years when the economy was growing quickly (Rosenberg 2010). Such development is worrisome for any advanced country.

Jordan

Jordan is a country with limited natural resources. Through continuous reforms, it has successfully created a favorable investment environment, in which businesses can flourish and prosper (Al-Mahrouq 2009). However, challenges still lie ahead with the main problems of oil imports and economic challenges.

Oil Imports

Jordan does not have oil fields and needs to rely on imports. Starting in 2005, Jordan's economy was negatively affected by the sharp increase of international oil prices. The effects of these factors were aggravated during the global financial crisis (Heritage 2012; Jaradat 2010). The country's trade balance is under the influence of its import bill and the fluctuation of regional demand. For example, after the crisis, Jordan had some problems finding alternatives to Egyptian gas supplies and the lower regional demand has also slowed its recovery (Barakat et al. 2012).

Economic Challenges

1. Jordan's ongoing problems include high budget deficit, high unemployment rate, high poverty level, and an influx of Iraqi refugees (Heritage 2012; Jaradat 2010). Therefore, the country needs to direct development project toward sectors that create more job opportunities.
2. The Jordanian government announced a 3-year fiscal reform agenda; however, the challenge lies in whether the following plans can be effectively implemented. They include minimizing vulnerabilities and spurring growth through boosting revenue, removing tax exemptions, revamping property transfer fees, and administering high tax rates on luxury goods (Barakat et al. 2012).
3. In Jordan, fundamental reforms are urgently needed to reach a stage where domestic revenues are sufficient to cover current expenditures, as capital expenditures are financed from borrowing or grants (Barakat et al. 2012).
4. Tourism activity and stagnating remittances are passively waiting for an easing of the regional situation (Barakat et al. 2012).
5. The government's desire to keep a tight rein on spending in 2011, in an effort to bring down the fiscal deficit, has been undermined by new commitments as a result of the domestic and regional political unrest (Barakat et al. 2012).

6. Jordan's banking sector is well known for its qualified financial professionals. However, the stakeholder survey indicated that 45 % of the banking businesses in Jordan see brain drain with the increasing migration of skilled and experienced employees (Al-Mahrouq 2009).
7. Extensive ICT use by SMEs and small family businesses needs to be further encouraged in order to strengthen their competitiveness.
8. Efforts to constantly improve public services and infrastructure are required.
9. Ensuring that education and training resources are in tune with and responsive to the needs of world-class business is important (Al-Mahrouq 2009).
10. Exploring new markets to reduce the external impact on exports is also needed.

South Africa

South Africa is below the worldwide average with respect to human development, economic freedom, and corruption (Heritage 2012). The most urgent problem is unemployment, which is coupled with weaknesses in the educational system and rather low productivity of the South African economy. Its future challenges may be described from the perspective of economic issues, poverty, unemployment, and environmental concern.

Economic Issues

1. South Africa's heavy dependence on financial flows into the stock market and the purchase of minerals is likely to erode its industrial base. During the financial crisis, several industrial sectors that had to be bailed out—such as the textile industry—demonstrated the need for structural change (Fakir 2009).
2. Since 2003, the current account deficit has continuously reached high levels, which raised concerns about its sustainability (Draper et al. 2009).
3. The financial crisis has highlighted the need for increasing potential growth through a combination of more counter-cyclical macroeconomic policy frameworks and structural reforms leading to higher employment, more competition on product markets, and greater innovation (OECD 2010). Making regulations less cumbersome is a promising option to boost entrepreneurship and innovation for long-term growth (Gurria 2010).
4. South Africa's lack of regulatory transparency still hinders investment (Heritage 2012). In addition, its outdated infrastructure has constrained growth (CIA 2012c). The government should tackle the bottlenecks in infrastructure, such as electricity, transport, and communication (Draper et al. 2009).
5. Despite South Africa's strong macroeconomic policy framework, job creation, and productivity growth remain too low to underpin sustained rapid GDP per

capita growth. The overarching challenge for South Africa is to boost its growth rate and create jobs (Gurria 2010).

6. Extreme unemployment interacting with other economic and social problems, such as inadequate education, poor health outcomes, and crime (Gurria 2010) slows down the country's economic development.
7. Cost competitiveness has been jeopardized by insider dominated wage bargaining. Government involvement in the process could help make the trade-offs between wages, employment, and unemployment clearer to social partners (Gurria 2010).
8. According to OECD, politically created barriers to market entry is a very important impediment for South Africa's further development. These barriers deter foreign investors and domestic entrepreneurs (Draper et al. 2009).
9. Productivity growth in South Africa has been rather mediocre and slower than in China and India. Government should address the problem of low productivity by fostering technological change and basic technologies through enhancing education policy at all levels (Draper et al. 2009).
10. A shift toward opening up financial industry to foreign competition would help upgrade the financial system (Draper et al. 2009).

Poverty

Progress in poverty reduction has been slow, as up to 73 % of sub-Saharan Africa's population still lived on $2 or less a day in 2008 compared to 76 % in 1990 (Ndikumana et al. 2010). The structural binds continue to trap people in South Africa in intergenerational poverty. Therefore, it is important to take rebound initiatives to favor the poor and employ some structural changes. Aligning industrial policy, labor market policies and skills policies to ensure an efficient matching of current and future demands should be considered (Frye 2009).

Unemployment

1. Extreme levels of unemployment have long characterized South Africa's economy (Assubuji et al. 2009; Draper et al. 2009; Gurria 2010). Unemployment in South Africa is very high, between 27 and 30 % in 2009 (Fakir 2009). At the time of the latest Income and Expenditure Survey (2005–2006), 63 % of youth between 15 and 30 were unemployed. Of these, 66 % (1.64 million people) had never before worked. Furthermore, youth constituted 74 % of the total number of officially unemployed people in 2005–2006. Therefore, within an overall employment strategy, measures should be targeted at tackling youth unemployment (OECD 2010).
2. More than a quarter of all working young people are employed in temporary positions with vulnerability (Frye 2009). Therefore, meaningful job creation,

encouragement of entrepreneurship, and wealth creation through a more sustainable growth path of the economy are needed to make full use of South Africa's large supply of underutilized human resources (Fakir 2009; OECD 2010).
3. Other important measures to raise employment over the long-term include improved basic education, reduced spatial mismatches between jobseekers and jobs, and better access to credit for small enterprises.

Environmental Concerns

1. South Africa scored relatively poorly on broad indices of environmental conditions, especially in the area of greenhouse gas emission. Better incentives would make the economy more environmentally sustainable (Gurria 2010; OECD 2010).
2. South Africa is predominantly agricultural and there is a water supply crisis. The use of surface water for irrigation in agriculture consumes approximately 60 % of the total available water annually, with the demand increasing every year (Blignaut 2009).
3. With critical electricity supply shortages, solving power supply challenges should be at the heart of South Africa's growth and development policy (Assubuji et al. 2009).
4. Rural communities can implement renewable energy (biomass and biogas technologies) and other "greening options," so that trade can be established in rural communities. These communities will then become part of the economic development process and solution, while the environment can be restored and become a contributing factor to the economy (Blignaut 2009).

Turkey

Turkey not only recovered from the financial crisis, but also thrived after the crisis. International rating agencies have great confidence in Turkey's future development. However, for Turkey to advance further, its challenges can be described from the perspectives of economic concerns, growth strategy, fiscal policy, and productivity and labor force.

Economic Concerns

1. Turkey's increase in the budget deficit and public debt requires improving budget balances in the medium term to stabilize debt. This should be achieved

via automatic stabilizers, a removal of recent discretionary measures and/or some additional tightening measures (Rawdanowicz 2010).
2. Turkey's regulatory regime, despite some improvements, remains burdensome and deters dynamic entrepreneurial activity; in addition, corruption is significant (Heritage 2012).
3. Turkish property rights are usually enforced, but the judiciary lacks efficiency and independence (Heritage 2012).
4. Turkey is emerging from the present crisis with a significantly higher level of unemployment and an appreciated real exchange rate (Rodrik 2009).
5. Turkey needs to export more for sustainable economic growth, which requires long-term and short-term structural reforms (Gursel 2011) .
6. Research and development is insufficiently supported and there is not enough diversification in exported products (Gursel 2011).
7. Further economic and judicial reforms are required to prepare for the prospective EU membership and to attract foreign investors (CIA 2012).

Growth Strategy

Turkey had good growth between 2002 and 2007, however such growth did not have much positive impact on unemployment, with the number of 10.5 % in 2003 versus 9.7 % by 2007 (Balaban 2009). This phenomenon has aroused attention regarding its growth strategy.

Turkey launched a mid-term growth strategy under the surveillance of the IMF and the World Bank, right after its 2000 economic crisis. However, the program was not sustainable from a long-term perspective, as it rested on high unemployment rates, low-cost labor, an increasing gap in income distribution, growing external deficit, an increasing current account deficit, privatization, poor fixed capital investment, and foreign capital inflows (Balaban 2009). In addition, Turkey came to rely increasingly on foreign borrowing to fuel its growth (Rodrik 2009). Since most of the financial inflows were mainly short-term investments, it is a highly unreliable source of growth (Balaban 2009). As a result, Turkish past growth lacked the solid elements of sustainability (Balaban 2009).

Although the Turkish economy grew at quite rapid rates in the years before this financial crisis, there were too many disconcerting elements in this growth experience (Rodrik 2009). In particular, domestic saving fell instead of rising and unemployment remained stubbornly high. The external deficit kept on widening and investment remained lower than required. All of these put the sustainability of the economic boom and the growth strategy into question (Rodrik 2009). The only alternative is to move to a growth model that breaks the link between growth and the current account deficit. However, if growth is going to be financed domestically, Turkey will need a permanently higher saving rate (Rodrik 2009).

Fiscal Policy

To increase domestic savings, the most direct way is to increase the structural surplus of the public sector. The medium term programs of the government must target a large enough fiscal surplus to leave room for the Central Bank to move interest rates to a permanently lower level. An increase in public saving will reduce capital inflows, prevent the current account deficit from rising, and help sustain a more competitive currency. This step should be a critical element in moving Turkey to a new growth path (Rodrik 2009).

Productivity and Labor Force

The Turkish economy has a serious productivity problem, which is closely related to labor force quality (Gursel 2011). Turkey's workforce is not well-educated and women's employment is low. Major educational reforms are needed, including upgrading teachers' qualifications (Gursel 2011). In Turkey, labor costs are also relatively high, which leads to low competitiveness on a global level (Gursel 2011).

Policy Implications

The 2008 financial crisis hit these four countries mainly through the drop of export demand and capital inflows due to the global inter-connectivity of trade and money market. Countries in this cluster held relatively conservative financial regulations without exposure to the complex financial instrument that paralyzed the western economies. Consequently, with relatively resilient financial system and free from housing price hike, economies of these countries rebounded fast (except Jordan) together with the recovery of the global economy in 2010. However, as the EU—one of their major trading partners—went into a second recession, growth of these four countries slowed down in 2011 and 2012, yet with steady recovery.

The prospect of countries in this cluster can be easily observed from the investors' confidence during the financial crisis, including foreign companies setting up R&D centers in Israel continuously, Arab customers regard Jordanian banks as a secured haven for their capital, increasing FDI inflows to South Africa in 2008, and international rating agencies rated Turkish bonds favorably. Examining the economic statuses of these four countries before, during, and after the financial crisis reveals important national policies, regulations, systems, and coping strategies that either facilitated or hampered the recovery. For example, talent retention policy in Israel facilitated its long-term development, while the Turkish growth strategy hampered it. These characteristics show that the intangibles—people, systems, governance, market dynamics, and the global interdependence—are the keys that caused this global financial catastrophe as well as future national development. National intellectual capital (NIC) represents a main part of national intangible assets. Research results reported in this booklet provide valuable information for the policy makers to look back on the national intangibles before the crisis, observe their co-development with GDP during and after the crisis, and then draw lessons from it.

By investigating the economic development and NIC development from 2005 to 2010, we have been able to connect the co-evolution of the tangibles and the intangibles for these four countries. Implications that can be drawn from our research findings are as follows:

First, national intellectual capital development goes together with the economic development and should be regarded as an enhancer of economic growth. The co-development of NIC and GDP with a high positive correlation (Fig. 3.7) indicates the higher the national intellectual capital the higher the GDP. That is, from our data of 48 countries, the intangible national intellectual capital development goes together with GDP growth. Figures 3.8–3.12 further exhibit the co-evolution of NIC and GDP for the four countries reported in this volume. For example, Jordan's relatively large scale decline in market capital, process capital, and renewal capital without rebound after the crisis (2009–2010) explain its weaker economic situation and slower recovery than the other three countries. An early sign of South Africa's problem before the financial crisis (stated in Chap. 2) was revealed from the short-term NIC scatterplot (Figure 3.15); its market capital had declined in 2006 and 2007 before the financial crisis. Therefore, attending to the development of NIC may help policy makers gain different perspectives on economic growth and pick up some early signs for timely national coping strategies.

Second, establishing a more effective national and NIC governance system to monitor national adherence to international financial standard is essential. Even though these four countries are gradually recovering from the financial crisis, some are still heavily in debt, such as Israel with its 77.3 % government debt in 2010 (Fig. 2.2). Therefore, establishing a more effective national and NIC governance system is essential. For example, regular monitoring of general government debt and deficit not to exceed 60 and 3 % of GDP, respectively and banking sector's capital adequacy rate based on Basel II or III rule will help the country build a more resilient economic system. In addition, governance to reduce the unemployment rate, especially youth unemployment should be a major task for countries with this chronic problem, such as South Africa. Jordan's NIC decline was connected to its weak economic development. Therefore, to reveal hidden risk that cannot be easily detected from national tangible assets (GDP related statistics), setting up a NIC governance system that continuously monitoring human capital, market capital, process capital, and renewal capital development may disclose important information for timely coping measures in this increasingly knowledge-oriented economy.

Third, national growth strategy needs to be revisited and refined for sustainable national and NIC development. This volume reveals some successful national growth strategies in the past have become a barrier for future sustainability. For example, with over a decade of development, Israel is very successful in its technology innovation start-ups, which bring large revenues to the country. However, critics commented that Israel's technology sector is relatively disconnected from broader domestic economic policy and cares little about local demand. So long as Israeli knowledge economy is concentrated narrowly on technology start-ups and then sold to Western countries without building a production or service base inside the country, Israel will continue to face problems of high unemployment, poverty, and income inequality (Rosenberg 2010). Besides, the country does not get the opportunity to develop the skills in marketing, finance, and managing a large organization. In addition to high social inequality of Israel, Table 3.1 also indicates that Israel ranked both number four in human capital and renewal capital among total 48 countries; yet, its financial capital ranked number 24 only. That is, Israeli strong human capital and R&D assets did not effectively translate to national wealth.

Turkey is another example. Turkey enjoyed a good growth between 2002 and 2007. However, the growth did not have a positive impact on unemployment, with less than 1 % unemployment rate reduction in 5 years. Critics commented that Turkish growth strategy rests on high unemployment rates, low-cost labor, an increasing gap in income distribution, growing external deficit, increasing current account deficit, poor fixed capital investment, and foreign capital inflows (Balaban 2009). Such development is unsustainable as indicated in its high unemployment issue after the financial crisis (over 10 %). Therefore, a revisit to Turkish growth strategies for a more long-lasting economic growth is essential. Furthermore, Jordan's past heavy reliance on external grants becomes more and more unsustainable, thus the country is enhancing its domestic financial support. The wake of a financial crisis is the best timing for national strategy modification and for sustainable national and NIC development.

Fourth, dependence on capital inflows needs to be gradually balanced by domestic financial support and NIC support. For emerging countries, international capital inflows facilitates national development is a proven successful model. Both South Africa and Turkey are clearly benefited from the FDI from foreign countries. However, during this financial crisis, many emerging economies were badly hurt by the sudden capital flights and the withdrawal of investment. In addition, this financial crisis also taught the export-dependent countries that developing domestic market development is very important to resist external shocks. Even China has announced that it will reduce exports and focus more on internal market development. South Africa and Turkey should have enough domestic consumers. For smaller economies like Israel and Jordan, semi-domestic market can be explored to expand its economic scale. For instance, Jordan's semi-domestic market could be its neighboring countries. For such national strategy transformation, national intellectual capital can play an important facilitating role. To build a stronger economy, sound tangible and intangible infrastructure are required, including roads, bridges, internet accessibility, government efficiency, and tax encouragement policy. While the tangible roads and transportation system are visible, the equally if not more important government policies are easily ignored. Our 3D NIC development trajectory indicates government related issues are major impeding factors of GDP growth in this country cluster. Such finding provides a good guidance for countries to have more focused investment in upgrading its intangible infrastructure as stated above.

Fifth, government needs to aggressively launch structural reforms for a more business-friendly and value creating internal as well as external environment. Following the concept that building a stronger domestic market is very important to resist external shock, structural reforms are needed to achieve that goal. During this financial crisis, countries recovered faster generally have stronger private sectors, as was the case in Israel and South Africa. To nurture more private sectors and energize the economy, government needs to provide facilitating policies. For example, Israeli government announced that its corporate tax will be gradually decreased from 24 % in 2011 to 18 % in 2016 to attract both foreign and domestic investors. In addition, our 3D NIC development trajectory unveils that government-related issues are the second major impeding factor (next to human capital in Table 3.3) to GDP growth. They include convenience of establishing new firms, corporate tax encouragement, fair business competition environment, government efficiency, corporate tax encouragement, and transparency of government policy. To promote more agile private industries, these are the areas that governments can launch reforms for future national economic development and well-being.

Sixth, export diversification can be pursued to spread financial risk with NIC support. During this financial crisis, export-dependent countries were hit the hardest, due to sudden drop of demand from the two major import regions—the U.S. and EU. Countries that have been gradually diversifying their export destinations fared better during the crisis, such as Israel. Its increased exports to Asia from 15 % in 2007 to 20 % in 2010, reduced its dependence on the EU market. East Asia and the BRIC (Brazil, Russia, India, and China) are expected to be the growth engine of future global economic development. Increasing trading with these countries should cast a promising prospect for a more balanced and risk-resilient export policy. With the diversification plan, improving the market capital related impeding factors summarized in Table 3.3 provides a good guideline for a more focused and efficient national investment. They include globalization, cross-border ventures, image of country, openness to culture, and export of goods.

Seventh, social partnership facilitates an economy to weather through the financial crisis and becomes valuable national process capital. During this financial crisis, both Israel and South Africa adopted the social partnership system that enables the government, business, community, and labor to work things out collaboratively. South Africa was particularly praised at the international level for bringing together social partners in forging a common response to the crisis. When such a system becomes a guideline for coping future national problems, it is an established government infrastructure (process capital) that promotes the well-being of the whole nation.

Eighth, capitalizing on national NIC strength is a sustainable way for future economic development and well-being. Each country has its own unique and strong intangible assets. For example, Israel excels in its renewal capital and human capital which enable the country to build its successful technology start-up industry. Jordan is known for its sound financial system in the Middle East and is fifth in the world for best medical tourism country. When comparing these two countries, it seems that Israel has been able to successfully capitalize its strength thus boost its economy. However, Jordan is not as successful as Israel in capitalizing its above stated unique resources, to the extent that it needs to rely on external grants to support its economy. Chapter 3 reports that Jordan lagged behind the other three countries in both NIC development and GDP growth. Jordan's relatively good human capital can further help sustain or even enhance its financial sector and medical tourism strengths for creating more values for the country. Its losing NIC international competitiveness (Figs. 3.19 and 3.20) provides a direction for Jordan to map its future coping strategies.

Ninth, retention of the talents is a challenging task that requires more NIC support. In looking at Israel, for example, the country is located in an unsecure region. Now that Israel relies heavily on the revenue generated by its technology industry, it worries about the talented people would leave the country to a better paid and safer place, such as Silicon Valley. To cope with this potential problem, Israeli government offers tax reduction to retain such kind of people and particularly openly promote the policy to attract global talents. Jordan also worries about the brain drain problem, especially in its financial sector. In nowadays global economy, human resource mobility to move to other countries becomes a lot easier. As a result, future competition is talent competition. A sound NIC system helps retain valuable people inside the national border. For instance, factors like convenience of establishing new firm, corporate tax encouragement, government efficiency, globalization, image of country, R&D investment, and the like may prompt a potential entrepreneur to stay in the country rather than going to a foreign place. Furthermore, the opportunity to work together with talents (human capital) in a globalized environment (market capital) with sound systems (process capital) entails the quality of work life. In other words, building a supportive environment including intangible attraction for private companies and talents to grow and thrive will be the key attractors to retain qualified people.

Concluding Remarks and Emerging Insights

The 2008 global financial crisis came with unexpected speed and magnitude. Fortunately, a great recession was avoided due to national and international measures that prevented the financial crisis from deteriorating. In the aftermath of the crisis, speed of recovery varies in different parts of the world. Countries reported in this volume have impressive recovery, except Jordan. According to the World Economic Forum 2011–2012 report, at the beginning of 2011, worldwide recovery appeared fairly certain, with economic growth for 2011 and 2012 projected by the international monetary fund (IMF) at 4.3 and 4.5 %, respectively. In the first quarter of 2012, global growth was 3.6 %. However, in the second quarter of 2012, growth momentum has slowed reflecting a weaker external environment.

Overall, global growth is projected to moderate to 3.5 % in 2012 and 3.9 % in 2013 (IMF 2012).

Economic developments in the past few years reinforce the observation that economic growth is unequally distributed which leads to the shift of economic activity away from the West. According to research, reducing public debt to precrisis levels will constrain government expenditures for at least a decade (World Economic Forum 2011) and on average, it takes four and a half years to get back to the same per capita GDP where a country started out and about the same amount of time for unemployment to stop rising (Rogoff 2011).

As a recap, to counter worsening economic conditions worldwide, a total of US$2 trillion stimulus packages, which amounts to approximately 3 % of world gross domestic product, have been allocated (some of the packages include measures that extend into subsequent years). The amount exceeded the call by the International Monetary Fund (IMF) for fiscal stimulus totaling 2 % of global GDP. IMF also estimated that as of January 2009, the U.S. fiscal stimulus packages as a percent of GDP in 2009 would amount to 1.9 %, for the euro area 0.9 %, for Japan 1.4 %, for Asia excluding Japan 1.5 % and for the rest of the G-20 countries 1.1 % (Nanto 2009).

Although there are early signs of problems in public statistics, they are largely neglected by countries seriously in trouble. In the wake of the crisis, a new surveillance mechanism is in place to initiate necessary procedure and propose economic sanctions on a member state whose structural imbalances are not corrected (IMF 2008). Alongside with planned structural reforms, macroeconomic, financial, and fiscal management would be strengthened in a more integrated way (Barnes 2010). Some countries have also been experimenting by creating an independent fiscal council to monitor and assess official fiscal projections. Furthermore, structural reform efforts were made to use more output-based performance measures and to choose the measures with care to avoid distorting incentives.

In terms of future NIC development, our other study on the top ten NIC ranking countries reveals that the interplay among the four capitals—human, market, process, and renewal—resulted in the best synergetic prospect for GDP growth. When their weaker capital (process capital) interacts with stronger capital (market capital), both effects on GDP are enhanced (Lin 2011). This finding prompts our suggestion for the countries to capitalize their strength for facilitating its future development. Overall, NIC intelligence suggests that in an era that the intangible asset has become a key competitive advantage, investing in national intellectual capital development is investing in future national development.

It is a fundamental function of government to create and maintain both tangible and intangible infrastructure under which the economic, social, and cultural life of the citizens can prosper. Since, it takes time to develop intangibles, countries that are determined to enhance their so-called soft-power need to consider the added value issue from the start of their policy making. The very origin of the financial crisis—people, systems, governance, market dynamics, and the global interdependence—is also the key to the economic recovery in any place and country.

Appendix 1
Summary of Stimulus and Relevant Packages of Israel, Jordan, South Africa, and Turkey

C. Y.-Y. Lin et al., *National Intellectual Capital and the Financial Crisis in Israel, Jordan, South Africa, and Turkey*, SpringerBriefs in Economics,
DOI: 10.1007/978-1-4614-7981-9, © The Author(s) 2014

Country	Date	Amount	Item
Israel	Nov 19, 2008	#1, #2 US$6.38bn (ILS25bn)	Other than developing desalination plants, doubling railway routes, increasing export credit, cutting assorted taxes, and creating aid packages to employers for hiring new workers, the stimulus package also included • US$2.5bn (ILS10bn) investment in infrastructure, beginning in 2010 • Credit lines for business, including US$45.2mn (ILS180mn) for small-sized businesses, US$251.3mn (ILS1bn) for medium-sized businesses and US$138.2mn (ILS550mn) for exporters • Additional spending of US$88mn (ILS350mn) on R&D and • Special funding for job retraining
	Apr 20, 2009	#3	An immediate 1 % cut in the corporate tax rate and a similar cut in personal income taxes
Jordan	Apr 2009	#4	• For loans at any of the country's commercial banks with the maximum interest rate of 8.5 %, beneficiaries paid 3.5 % of the interest and the government covered the rest • Extend the maturity period of loans with local banks from 20 to 25 years • Bank loans would cover 100 % of the cost of the house and increase the monthly installment deduction from 40 % currently to 50 %, from the beneficiaries' monthly income
South Africa	Feb 2008	#5 US$69bn	Infrastructural expenditure plan
	Jan 2009	#5 US$14.81 mn	Development bank of Southern Africa provided Airports Company South Africa with financial assistance
	Feb 11, 2009	#6	• Poverty reduction: US$2.5bn (ZAR25bn) was added to the budgets of provinces, mainly for education and health care, and US$1.3bn (ZAR13bn) for social assistance grants and their administration. US$404mn (ZAR4bn) was added to the school nutrition program and US$252.5mn (ZAR2.5bn) went to municipalities for basic services • Accelerate employment growth: Government worked with business and organized labor to protect work opportunities and accelerate skills development. Additional funding for the Working for Water and Working on Fire programs, and US$101mn (ZAR1bn) went to the Umsobomvu Youth Fund. US$373.7mn (ZAR3.7bn) was added for low-income housing projects and US$414.1mn (ZAR4.1bn) was set aside for the second phase of the expanded public works program • Building capacity to grow: US$79.5bn (ZAR787bn) infrastructure investment plans. In this budget a further US$646.4mn (ZAR6.4bn) was added for public transport, roads and rail networks, US$414.1mn (ZAR4.1bn) for school buildings, clinics and other provincial infrastructure projects, and US$535.3mn (ZAR5.3bn) for municipal infrastructure and bulk water systems • Address regulatory and microeconomic barriers to competitiveness: US$161.6mn (ZAR1.6bn) was added to industrial development and small enterprise support programs, and US$181.8mn (ZAR1.8bn) went to rural development and small farmer support. A further US$101mn (ZAR1bn) was added for electricity demand management, together with tax incentives for investment in energy efficient technologies • Sustainability of the public finances

(continued)

(continued)

Country	Date	Amount	Item
	Apr 2009	#7	South Africa tripled its resources available to the IMF, to US$750bn, and supported a new special drawing rights (SDR) allocation of US$250bn, an additional US$100bn in lending from the multilateral development banks, ensuring US$250bn for trade finance and using additional resources derived from the sale of IMF gold for concessional finance for the poorest countries
	Oct 2011	#8 US$3.2bn	A competitiveness support package over the next 6 years to boost industrial development, assist enterprises and accelerate job creation
Turkey	Feb 18, 2009	#9	Reduced corporate tax on investment, cut taxes on textiles and clothing manufacturers if they moved their plants to certain cities Encouraged people to scrap old cars to boost sales of new vehicles among Turkey's auto manufacturing sector
	Mar 6, 2009	#10 US$9.84bn (TRY17bn)	Financial support for companies to curb lay-offs and expand infrastructure spending
	Mar 13, 2009	#11 US$3.2bn (TRY5.5bn)	• Temporary tax cuts for 3 months in the housing, home appliances, and automotive sectors • Lowered the private consumption tax rates on the automotive sector and remove such rate completely on home appliances • The value added tax (VAT) on apartments over 150 m^2 (1,614 square feet) in size was lowered from 18 to 8 %
		US$296mn (TRY500mn)	• Allocated an additional US$296mn (TRY500mn) to Exim bank, a state-owned bank to support exporters

#1. Asa-El A (2008) Israel's bizarre economic-stimulus saga. Mark Watch. Retrieved from http://articles.marketwatch.com/2008-11-28/news/30765595_1_stimulus-packages-howitzer

#2. Oxford Analytica (2008) Israel's stimulus plan draws protest. Forbes. Retrieved from http://www.forbes.com/2008/11/24/israel-financial-crisis-cx_1125oxford.html

#3. Sandler N (2009) Netanyahu unveils Israeli stimulus plan. Bloomberg Bus Week. Retrieved from http://www.businessweek.com/globalbiz/content/apr2009/gb20090423_881455.htm

#4. Jordan Times (2009) Jordan-Government stimulus targets housing initiative. Menafn. Retrieved from http://www.menafn.com/qn_news_story_s.asp?StoryId=1093244808

#5. Economy Watch (2010) South Africa economic stimulus package. Retrieved from http://www.economywatch.com/economic-stimulus-package/south-africa.html

#6. Manuel TA (2009) 2009 budget speech. Retrieved from http://www.treasury.gov.za/documents/national%20budget/2009/speech/speech.pdf

#7. Dlamini T (2010) South Africa country report. In: Stiftung B (ed) Managing the Crisis. A Comparative Assessment of Economic Governance in 14 Economies. Bertelsmann Stiftung, Gütersloh, 2010. Retrieved from http://www.bertelsmann-transformation-index.de/pdf/South_Africa.pdf

#8. Gerardy J (2011) South Africa to launch $3.2bn stimulus package. Afr Rev. Retrieved from http://www.africareview.com/Business+++Finance/-/979184/1261984/-/115wckyz/-/index.html

#9. Reuters (2009a) Turkey parliament approves stimulus package-report. Retrieved from http://in.reuters.com/article/2009/02/18/turkey-economy-package-idINLI34137920090218

#10. Reuters (2009b) Turkey stimulus to cost 17 bln lira—deputy PM. World Bull. Retrieved from http://www.worldbulletin.net/index.php?aType=haberArchive&ArticleID=37772

#11. Kardas S (2009) Turkish economic stimulus package foresees temporary tax cuts in automotive and other sectors. Eurasia Daily Monit (6.50). Retrieved from http://www.jamestown.org/programs/edm/single/?tx_ttnews%5Btt_news%5D=34713&tx_ttnews%5BbackPid%5D=485&no_cache=1

Appendix 2
Important Meetings Held by World Leaders to Address the 2008 Global Financial Crisis

Date	Place	
June 18–19	Los Cabos, Mexico	G20
March 1–2, 2012	Brussels	European Council
January 30, 2012	Brussels	Informal meeting of members of the European council
December 8, 2011	Brussels	European council
November 12–13, 2011	Honolulu, USA	19th APEC economic leaders' meeting
November 3–4, 2011	Cannes, France	G20
October 23, 2011	Brussels	European council
September 10, 2011	Marseille	G8 Deauville partnership finance ministers
September 9–10, 2011	Marseille	G7 finance ministers and central bank governors
July 21, 2011	Brussels	Meeting of heads of state or government of the Euro area
June 23–24, 2011	Brussels	European council
March 24–25, 2011	Brussels	European council
March 17, 2011	Japan	G7 finance ministers telephone conference
March 11, 2011	Brussels	extraordinary European council
February 4, 2011	Brussels	European council
December 16–17, 2010	Brussels	European council
November 21, 2010	Ireland	G7 finance ministers
November 13–14, 2010	Yokohama, Japan	18th APEC economic leaders' meeting
November 11–12, 2010	Seoul, Korea	G20
October 28–29, 2010	Brussels	European council
October 8, 2010	Washington DC	G7 finance ministers and central bank governors
September 16, 2010	Brussels	European council
June 26–27, 2010	Toronto, Canada	G20
June 17, 2010	Brussels	European council
March 25–26, 2010	Brussels	European council
February 11, 2010	Brussels	Informal meeting of heads of state or government of the European union

(continued)

C. Y.-Y. Lin et al., *National Intellectual Capital and the Financial Crisis in Israel, Jordan, South Africa, and Turkey*, SpringerBriefs in Economics,
DOI: 10.1007/978-1-4614-7981-9,

(continued)

Date	Place	
February 5–6, 2010	Iqaluit, Nunavut, Canada	G7 finance ministers and central bank governors
December 10–11, 2009	Brussels	European council
November 19, 2009	Brussels	Informal meeting of heads of state or government of the European union
November 14–15, 2009	Singapore	17th APEC economic leaders' meeting
October 29–30, 2009	Brussels	European council
October 3, 2009	Istanbul, Turkey	G7 finance ministers and central bank governors
September 24–25, 2009	Pittsburgh, USA	G20
September 17, 2009	Brussels	Informal meeting of heads of state or government of the European union
June 18–19, 2009	Brussels	European Council
June 12–13, 2009	Lecce, Italy	G8 finance ministers
April 24, 2009	Washington DC	G7 finance ministers and central bank governors
April 2, 2009	G20 London Summit United Kingdom	G20
March 19–20, 2009	Brussels	European council
February 2009	Rome	G7 finance ministers and central bank governors
December 11–12, 2008	Brussels	European council
November 2008	G20 APEC Peru	G20
November 22–23, 2008	Lima, Peru	16th APEC economic leaders' meeting
November 14–15, 2008	Washington DC., USA	G7
October 15–16, 2008	Brussels	European council
October 10, 2008	Washington, DC	G7 finance ministers
September 1, 2008	Brussels	Extraordinary European council
July 7–9, 2008	Tokyo, Japan	34th G8 summit
June 19–20, 2008	Brussels	European council
June 13–14, 2008	Osaka	G8 finance ministers meeting
March 13–14, 2008	Brussels	European council
February 9, 2008	Tokyo	G7 finance ministers and central bank governors meeting

For further information
http://g20mexico.org/en/g20/previous-leaders-summits
http://www.g8.utoronto.ca/finance/index.htm
http://video.consilium.europa.eu/ecofin/
http://www.european-council.europa.eu/council-meetings/conclusions
http://www.apec.org/

Appendix 3
Indicators in Each Type of Capital

Human capital index	*Market capital index*
1.Skilled labor*	1. Corporate tax*
2.Employee training*	2. Cross-border venture*
3.Literacy rate	3. Openness of culture*
4.Higher education enrollment	4. Globalization*
5.Pupil-teacher ratio	5. Transparency*
6.Internet subscribers	6. Image of country*
7.Public expenditure on education	7. Exports of goods
Process capital index	*Renewal capital index*
1.Business competition environment*	1.Business R&D spending
2.Government efficiency*	2.Basic research*
3.Intellectual property rights protection*	3.R&D spending/GDP
4.Capital availability*	4.R&D researchers
5.Computers in use per capita	5.Cooperation between universities and enterprises*
6.Convenience of establishing new firms*	6.Scientific articles
7.Mobile phone subscribers	7.Patents per capita (USPTO + EPO)

Remarks
1. Financial capital is the logarithm of GDP per capita adjusted by purchasing power parity.
2. Indicators marked with an asterisk (*) are rated qualitatively using a scale of 1–10.
3. Indicators with objective numbers are transformed to 1-10 scores, by calculating the ratio to the highest number in that indicator and then multiply 10.
4. Readers can refer to the book National Intellectual Capital: A comparison of 40 countries for model validation details (www.nic40.org)

C. Y.-Y. Lin et al., *National Intellectual Capital and the Financial Crisis in Israel, Jordan, South Africa, and Turkey*, SpringerBriefs in Economics,
DOI: 10.1007/978-1-4614-7981-9,

Appendix 4
Definition of the 29 Indicators

Indicators	Definition
Human capital	
Skilled labor*	Whether skilled labor is readily available
Employee training*	Whether employee training is a high propriety in companies
Literacy rate	Adult (over 15 years) literacy rate as a percentage of population
Higher education enrollment	Percentage of population that has attained at least tertiary education
Pupil-teacher ratio	Ratio of teaching staff to students
Internet subscribers	Number of internet users per 1000 people
Public expenditure on education	Total public expenditure on education (percentage of GDP)
Market capital	
Corporate tax encouragement*	Whether corporate taxes encourage entrepreneurial activity
Cross-border venture*	Whether international transactions can be freely negotiated with foreign partners
Openness to foreign culture*	Whether the national culture is open to foreign culture ideas
Attitudes toward globalization*	Whether attitudes toward globalization are generally positive in a given society
Transparency*	Whether transparency of government policy is satisfactory
Country image*	Whether the image abroad of a given country encourages business development
Exports of goods	Exports of goods (Percentage of GDP)
Process capital	
Business competition environment*	Whether competition legislation is efficient in preventing unfair competition
Government efficiency*	Whether government bureaucracy hinders business activity
Intellectual property rights protection*	Whether intellectual property rights are adequately enforced
Capital availability*	Whether cost of capital encourages business development
Computers in use per capita	Number of computers per 1,000 people

(continued)

C. Y.-Y. Lin et al., *National Intellectual Capital and the Financial Crisis in Israel, Jordan, South Africa, and Turkey*, SpringerBriefs in Economics,
DOI: 10.1007/978-1-4614-7981-9, © The Author(s) 2014

(continued)

Indicators	Definition
Convenience of establishing new firms*	Whether creation of firms is supported by legislation
Mobile phone subscribers	Number of subscribers per 1,000 inhabitants
Renewal capital	
Business R&D spending	Business expenditure on R&D (per capita)
Basic research*	Whether basic research enhances long-term economic development
R&D spending/GDP	Total expenditure on R&D (percentage of GDP)
R&D researchers	Total R&D personnel nationwide per capita (Full-time work equivalent per 1,000 people)
Cooperation between universities and enterprises*	Whether knowledge transfer is highly developed between universities and companies
Scientific articles	Scientific articles published by origin of author (per capita)
Patents per capita (USPTO + EPO)	USPTO and EPO total patents granted (per capita)
Financial capital	
GDP per capita (PPP) (From IMF)	Gross domestic product based on purchasing-power-parity (PPP) per capita

Appendix 5
48 Countries by Country Cluster and by Continent

This booklet series cover a total of 48 countries. Eleven country clusters and country coverage are displayed hereunder for readers' reference. China, Brazil, and South Africa are grouped twice to maintain cluster completeness; that is, China is in both Greater China region and BRICKS region, Brazil is in both BRICKS region and Latin American region, and South Africa is in both BRICKS region and Cluster 5.

Eleven country clusters

1. Portugal, Italy, Greece, Spain
2. Greater China region (China, Hong Kong, Singapore, Taiwan)
3. Brazil, Russia, India, China, Korea, South Africa (BRICKS)
4. Indonesia, Malaysia, the Philippines, Thailand
5. Israel, Jordan, Turkey, South Africa
6. Bulgaria, Czech Republic, Hungary, Romania, Poland
7. Austria, Belgium, the Netherlands, Switzerland
8. France, Germany, Ireland, United Kingdom
9. Argentina, Brazil, Chile, Colombia, Mexico, Venezuela
10. Australia, Canada, Japan, New Zealand, USA
11. Denmark, Finland, Iceland, Norway, Sweden

Europe: 24 countries

Nordic Europe: Denmark, Finland, Iceland, Norway, and Sweden
Western Europe: Austria, Belgium, France, Germany, Ireland, Netherlands, Switzerland, and UK
Southern Europe: Greece, Italy, Portugal, and Spain
Eastern Europe: Russia
East Central Europe: Bulgaria, Czech Republic, Hungary, Poland, Romania, and Turkey

C. Y.-Y. Lin et al., *National Intellectual Capital and the Financial Crisis in Israel, Jordan, South Africa, and Turkey*, SpringerBriefs in Economics,
DOI: 10.1007/978-1-4614-7981-9, © The Author(s) 2014

Americas: 8 countries

North America: Canada, USA
Latin America: Argentina, Brazil, Chile, Colombia, Mexico, and Venezuela

Australia: 2 countries

Australia and New Zealand

Asia: 13 countries

East Asia: China, Hong Kong, Japan, Korea, and Taiwan.
West Asia: Israel, Jordan.
Southeast Asia: Indonesia, Malaysia, Philippines, Singapore, and Thailand.
South Asia: India

Africa: 1 country

South Africa

Appendix 6
National Intellectual Capital Scores and Ranking Comparison for 48 Countries (2005–2010)

C. Y.-Y. Lin et al., *National Intellectual Capital and the Financial Crisis in Israel, Jordan, South Africa, and Turkey*, SpringerBriefs in Economics,
DOI: 10.1007/978-1-4614-7981-9, © The Author(s) 2014

2005-2010	Human capital		Market capital		Process capital		Renewal capital		Financial capital		NIC	
Mean	6.420		5.409		5.345		3.658		9.115		29.946	
SD	1.217		1.085		1.454		2.056		0.690		5.840	
Country	Score	Ranking	Score	Ranking	Score	Ranking	Score	Ranking	Score	Ranking	Score	Ranking
Argentina	5.370	36	3.340	47	3.038	47	1.413	45	8.755	34	21.916	45
Australia	7.205	15	6.199	12	6.938	9	4.927	16	9.695	11	34.964	13
Austria	7.229	14	6.203	11	6.982	8	5.296	12	9.708	10	35.418	11
Belgium	7.666	8	5.519	23	5.924	21	4.706	17	9.635	14	33.450	19
Brazil	4.757	44	4.589	38	3.076	46	1.753	36	8.481	40	22.656	42
Bulgaria	5.493	34	4.929	31	4.054	36	1.589	41	8.646	37	24.710	35
Canada	7.855	6	6.137	13	6.464	15	5.064	14	9.710	9	35.229	12
Chile	5.414	35	6.663	5	5.163	28	1.710	37	8.784	32	27.734	30
China	4.942	39	5.184	28	3.746	40	2.099	33	7.967	44	23.938	40
Colombia	4.941	40	4.677	36	3.951	37	1.435	44	8.348	42	23.352	41
Czech Republic	5.995	30	5.720	18	5.378	25	2.905	24	9.271	27	29.269	25
Denmark	8.545	1	6.662	6	7.642	1	6.587	6	9.665	13	39.101	3
Finland	7.601	9	6.232	10	7.399	3	7.755	3	9.606	17	38.593	4
France	6.956	20	4.141	45	5.730	22	4.500	20	9.585	18	30.912	23
Germany	6.761	23	5.630	19	6.489	14	5.796	9	9.612	16	34.287	17
Greece	5.986	31	4.216	43	4.113	35	2.168	32	9.440	23	25.923	31
Hong Kong	6.564	25	8.090	2	7.209	5	3.277	23	9.794	4	34.934	14
Hungary	6.674	24	4.836	32	5.095	29	2.301	29	9.046	29	27.952	29
Iceland	8.357	3	5.614	21	6.561	12	5.931	8	9.713	8	36.154	8
India	3.926	48	5.620	20	3.556	42	1.954	34	7.285	48	22.340	44
Indonesia	4.062	47	4.832	33	3.257	44	1.519	42	7.594	46	21.263	47
Ireland	7.145	16	6.816	3	6.711	11	4.101	21	9.768	5	34.541	16
Israel	8.040	4	5.954	16	6.454	17	7.091	4	9.414	24	36.953	6
Italy	6.471	28	4.155	44	5.184	27	2.745	26	9.479	22	28.035	28
Japan	7.581	10	4.820	34	6.209	18	6.473	7	9.576	19	34.659	15
Jordan	5.345	37	5.341	26	4.411	32	2.212	30	7.865	45	25.174	33
Korea	6.964	19	5.123	29	5.282	26	4.595	19	9.383	25	31.348	22

(continued)

(continued)

2005-2010	Human capital		Market capital		Process capital		Renewal capital		Financial capital		NIC	
Mean	6.420		5.409		5.345		3.658		9.115		29.946	
SD	1.217		1.085		1.454		2.056		0.690		5.840	
Country	Score	Ranking	Score	Ranking	Score	Ranking	Score	Ranking	Score	Ranking	Score	Ranking
Malaysia	6.538	26	6.410	9	5.567	23	2.186	31	8.740	35	29.442	24
Mexico	4.871	42	4.491	39	3.226	45	1.237	48	8.781	33	22.606	43
Netherlands	7.312	12	6.761	4	6.879	10	5.163	13	9.739	7	35.855	10
New Zealand	7.123	18	5.999	15	6.460	16	3.701	22	9.380	26	32.662	21
Norway	7.936	5	6.055	14	7.008	7	4.961	15	9.987	1	35.947	9
Philippines	4.772	43	4.464	40	3.317	43	1.268	47	7.481	47	21.302	46
Poland	6.393	29	4.246	41	3.895	38	1.819	35	8.945	30	25.299	32
Portugal	6.882	22	4.801	35	5.470	24	2.467	27	9.224	28	28.844	26
Romania	5.829	32	4.219	42	3.806	39	1.685	38	8.594	39	24.133	39
Russia	5.530	33	3.860	46	3.588	41	2.349	28	8.822	31	24.150	38
Singapore	7.144	17	8.306	1	7.506	2	5.416	11	9.961	2	38.334	5
South Africa	4.708	45	4.976	30	4.472	31	1.677	39	8.472	41	24.306	37
Spain	6.524	27	4.649	37	5.033	30	2.787	25	9.484	21	28.476	27
Sweden	8.385	2	6.563	7	7.174	6	7.780	2	9.673	12	39.575	1
Switzerland	7.575	11	6.481	8	7.374	4	7.988	1	9.753	6	39.172	2
Taiwan	7.244	13	5.823	17	6.026	20	5.425	10	9.526	20	34.044	18
Thailand	5.310	38	5.524	22	4.365	33	1.436	43	8.304	43	24.938	34
Turkey	4.703	46	5.227	27	4.167	34	1.666	40	8.690	36	24.453	36
United Kingdom	6.939	21	5.440	24	6.090	19	4.697	18	9.626	15	32.793	20
USA	7.695	7	5.348	25	6.558	13	6.715	5	9.886	3	36.202	7
Venezuela	4.884	41	2.761	48	2.545	48	1.277	46	8.625	38	20.092	48

Appendix 7
Country Profile: Additional Statistics

1. **International reserves in millions of US$**

Country	2005	2006	2007	2008	2009	2010
Israel	27,155	28,047	30,627	29,539	44,327	62,464
Jordan	5,317	5,395	7,032	6,117	9,214	11,899
South Africa	14,148	20,607	23,849	30,615	30,376	37,496
Turkey	38,232	58,549	67,434	76,583	67,418	69,411

Source: Global Finance http://www.gfmag.com/

2. **Real GDP growth_% change**

Country	2005	2006	2007	2008	2009	2010
Israel	4.9	5.6	5.5	4.0	0.8	4.8
Jordan	8.1	8.1	8.2	7.2	5.5	2.3
South Africa	5.3	5.6	5.6	3.6	−1.7	2.8
Turkey	8.4	6.9	4.7	0.7	−4.8	8.9

Source: World Economic Outlook Database http://www.imf.org/external/ns/cs.aspx?id=28

3. **GDP per capita (PPP)_current international dollar**

Country	2005	2006	2007	2008	2009	2010
Israel	24,223	25,975	27,554	28,715	28,581	29,531
Jordan	4,289	4,672	5,105	5,492	5,548	5,644
South Africa	8,654	9,336	10,049	10,453	10,238	10,498
Turkey	11,006	12,107	12,901	13,124	12,466	13,464

Source: World Economic Outlook Database http://www.imf.org/external/ns/cs.aspx?id=28

C. Y.-Y. Lin et al., *National Intellectual Capital and the Financial Crisis in Israel, Jordan, South Africa, and Turkey*, SpringerBriefs in Economics,
DOI: 10.1007/978-1-4614-7981-9, © The Author(s) 2014

4. GDP (PPP)—share of world total_%

Country	2005	2006	2007	2008	2009	2010
Israel	0.29	0.29	0.29	0.29	0.30	0.30
Jordan	0.04	0.04	0.04	0.05	0.05	0.05
South Africa	0.72	0.72	0.72	0.73	0.72	0.71
Turkey	1.32	1.34	1.33	1.31	1.26	1.30

Source: World Economic Outlook Database http://www.imf.org/external/ns/cs.aspx?id=28

5. Gross domestic expenditure on R&D as a % of GDP

Country	2005	2006	2007	2008	2009	2010
Israel	4.55	4.71	4.48	4.68	4.86	4.27
Jordan	0.81	0.74	0.75	0.75	0.75	0.51
South Africa	0.73	0.78	0.92	0.92	0.95	0.92
Turkey	0.66	0.67	0.59	0.58	0.72	0.85

Source: IMD World Competitiveness Yearbook 2006–2011

Glossary

Basel II Basel II is the second of the Basel Accords, which are recommendations on banking laws and regulations issued by the Basel Committee on banking supervision. Basel II, initially published in June 2004, was intended to create an international standard for banking regulators to control how much capital banks need to put aside to guard against the types of financial and operational risks banks face, 8% ratio usually recommended by the Basel agreements.

BBC British Broadcasting Corporation

BSEC Black Sea Economic Cooperation (BSEC) region

Cap and trade Cap and trade is an environmental policy tool that delivers results with a mandatory cap on emissions while providing sources flexibility in how they comply

CIA The U.S. Central Intelligence Agency

CPI Consumer price inflation

CSIS Center for Strategic & International Studies

ERfKE Education Reform for Knowledge Economy (ERfKE) in Jordan

EU European Union

ETS Emission trading system

FC Financial capital

FDI Foreign direct investment

FTA Free trade agreement

GCI Global Competitiveness Index (published by World Economic Forum)

GDP Gross domestic product

GDP per capita (PPP) Gross domestic product per capita adjusted by purchasing power parity

C. Y.-Y. Lin et al., *National Intellectual Capital and the Financial Crisis in Israel, Jordan, South Africa, and Turkey*, SpringerBriefs in Economics,
DOI: 10.1007/978-1-4614-7981-9,

HC Human capital

IDR Issuer Default Rating (Fitch rating)

IMD International Institute for Management Development

IMF International Monetary Fund

IP Intellectual Property

JOD Jordanian dinar (currency)

Long-term NIC Long-term oriented national intellectual capital, represented by human capital and renewal capital

MC Market capital

NEDLAC National Economic Development and Labor Council in South Africa

NIC National intellectual capital

OECD Organization for Economic Cooperation and Development

PC Process capital

PPP Purchasing power parity

R&D Research and development

RC Renewal capital

Short-term NIC Short-term oriented national intellectual capital, represented by market capital and process capital

SMEs Small and Medium-sized Enterprises

S&P Standard & Poor (rating company)

Term of trade Term of trade means what quantity of imports can be purchased through the sale of a fixed quantity of exports

Three time periods For the convenience of comparing ranking changes, the 6 years data were separated into three time periods, namely 2005–2006, 2007–2008, and 2009–2010. Two years each represents "before, during, and after" the 2008 global financial crisis. Even though Euro zone is still in sovereign debt trouble as of mid-2012, the time partition is based on the financial crisis progression in the epicenter. The signs of financial trouble appeared in 2007 and the crisis was declared over in the third quarter of 2009.

Tier 1 capital Tier I capital is core capital, including disclosed reserves and equity capital, which cannot be redeemed at the option of the holder.

UNCTAD United Nations Conference on Trade and Development

USPTO United States Patent and Trademark Office

VAT Value-added tax

WEF World Economic Forum that ranked Global Competitiveness Index (GCI)

WTO World Trade Organization

References

Ali S (2011) Jordan: looking towards the GCC, in Fragile West, resilient East, Global Focus-2012. Stand Chartered Glob Res. Retrieved from http://www.privatebank.standardchartered.com/_pdf/en/Global%20Focus%202012.pdf

Alnajjar F, Noor M, Al-ahmad N, Issa S (2011) The global financial crisis and its impact on the financial sector in Jordan: applied study on financial companies listed in Amman stock exchange. Retrieved from http://www.uop.edu.jo/download/research/members/285_1968_Faye.pdf

Al-Mahrouq M (2009) Jordan's national competitiveness report 2008–2009: entering a new era of global competitiveness. Policies and Studies Department, Ministry of Planning and International Cooperation, Jordan. Retrieved from http://www.amman.polemb.net/gallery/serwis/header/DoingBusiness/PolandCloser/2009/JORDAN1.pdf

Altman RC. (2009) The great crash, 2008: a geopolitical setback for the west, Foreign Affair. Retrieved from http://www.foreignaffairs.com/articles/63714/roger-c-altman/the-great-crash-2008

Ammon News (2009) Economists, officials see Jordan's recovery from economic crisis in different ways. Retrieved from http://en.ammonnews.net/article.aspx?articleNO=4202

Assubuji P, Luckscheiter J, and Ben-Zeev K (eds) (2009) The global economic crisis and South Africa. Perspectives, #3.09. Polit Anal Commentary South Afr. Retrieved from http://www.boell.org.za/downloads/Perspectives_3-09.pdf

Babacan A (2009) Global financial crisis and the Turkish economy. Minister of State and Deputy Prime Minister speech invited by London School of Economics European Institute. Retrieved from http://www2.lse.ac.uk/publicEvents/pdf/20090917_AliBabacan.pdf

Balaban NB (2009) Global economic crisis and Turkey. Commentary, Turkish Yearb Int Relat V. 40. Retrieved from http://dergiler.ankara.edu.tr/dergiler/44/1566/17009.pdf

Barakat MS, Naayem JH, Baba SS, Kanso FA, and Ghorayeb NF (2012) Jordan economic report: challenging twin deficits in a "wait and see" mode economy. Bank Audi sal, Audi Saradar Group, Group Research Department. Retrieved from http://research.banqueaudi.com/documents/EconomicReports/jordan_economic_report.pdf

Barnes S (2010) OECD economic surveys: Euro area 2010, resolving and avoiding unsustainable imbalances. Economics Department, working paper No. 827. Retrieved from http://www.keepeek.com/Digital-Asset-Management/oecd/economics/oecd-economic-surveys-euro-area-2010/resolving-and-avoiding-unsustainable-imbalances_eco_surveys-euz-2010-5-en

Baxter R (2012) The global economic crisis and its impact on South Africa and the country's mining industry. South Afr Reserve Bank. Retrieved from http://www.resbank.co.za/Lists/News%20and%20Publications/Attachments/51/Roger+Baxter.pdf in May 2012

C. Y.-Y. Lin et al., *National Intellectual Capital and the Financial Crisis in Israel, Jordan, South Africa, and Turkey*, SpringerBriefs in Economics,
DOI: 10.1007/978-1-4614-7981-9,

Blignaut J (2009) South Africa and sustainable development: a reflection. In: Assubuji P, Luckscheiter J, Ben-Zeev K (eds) Perspectives, #3.09. Retrieved from http://www.boell.org.za/downloads/Perspectives_3-09.pdf

Brosh S (ed) (2011) The Israeli economy and the global economic crisis. Fed Israeli Econ Organ. Retrieved from http://www.industry.org.il/_UploadsCl/dbsAttachedFiles/m11211.pdf

Buchwald D (2009) Israel and the global economic crisis. Focus Q. Retrieved from http://www.jewishpolicycenter.org/969/israel-global-economic-crisis

CIA (2012) Israel. Retrieved from https://www.cia.gov/library/publications/the-world-factbook/geos/th.html

Draper P, Freytag A, Voll S (2009) Global financial crisis, protectionism and current account deficit: South Africa on the brink? Working paper No. 8, Global Financial Markets, University Jena and University Halle. Retrieved from http://pubdb.wiwi.uni-jena.de/pdf/wp_hlj08-2009.pdf

Edvinsson L, Malone MS (1997) Intellectual capital: realizing your company's true value by finding its hidden brainpower. Harper Business, New York

Elman A (2011) Understanding the Israeli economic crisis, and the opportunity. The Algemeine. Retrieved from http://www.algemeiner.com/2011/08/05/understanding-the-israeli-economic-crisis-and-the-opportunity/

Fackler M (2008) Financial crisis spreads to emerging nations. The New York Times. Retrieved from http://www.nytimes.com/2008/10/24/business/worldbusiness/24won.html

Fakir S (2009) Caught between a rock and hard place: the state of play for South Africa's beleaguered development state. In: Assubuji P, Luckscheiter J, Ben-Zeev K (eds) Perspectives, #3.09. Retrieved from http://www.boell.org.za/downloads/Perspectives_3-09.pdf

Friedberg R (2009) Economic highlights: 4th Quarter 2008. State of Israel, Ministry of Finance, International Affairs Department. Retrieved from http://eng.mni.gov.il/FinanceIsrael/Docs/En/EconomicHighlights/EconomicHighlights-2008-4.pdf

Frye I (2009) Responses and alternatives: South Africa's response to the crisis. In: Assubuji P, Luckscheiter J, Ben-Zeev K (eds) Perspectives, #3.09. Retrieved from http://www.boell.org.za/downloads/Perspectives_3-09.pdf

Gonene R, Sahinoz S, Tuncel O (2010) Turkey's improving integration with the global capital market: impacts on risk premia and capital costs. OECD, Economic Department Working Paper No. 812. Retrieved from http://www.oecd.org/officialdocuments/displaydocumentpdf/?cote=eco/wkp(2010)68&doclanguage=en

Gurria A (2010) Economic survey of South Africa 2010. OECD. Retrieved from http://www.oecd.org/document/21/0,3746,en_2649_34571_45637781_1_1_1_1,00.html

Global Finance (2012a) Data on GDP and economic information: Israel. Retrieved from http://www.gfmag.com/gdp-data-country-reports/250-israel-gdp-country-report.html#axzz1urt0NIn8

Global Finance (2012b) Data on GDP and economic information: South Africa. Retrieved from http://www.gfmag.com/gdp-data-country-reports/176-south-africa-gdp-country-report.html#axzz1urt0NIn8

Global Finance (2012c) Data on GDP and economic information: Turkey. Retrieved from http://www.gfmag.com/gdp-data-country-reports/157-turkey-gdp-country-report.html#axzz1urt0NIn8

Gursel S (2011) Can Turkey limit effects of another financial crisis in Europe? Bus Turkey Today. Retrieved from http://www.businessturkeytoday.com/can-turkey-limit-effects-of-another-financial-crisis-in-europe/

Heritage Foundation (2012) Economic freedom. Retrieved from http://www.heritage.org

International Labor Office (ILO) (2010a) G20 country briefs: South Africa's response to the crisis. G20 Meeting of Labor and Employment Ministers, Washington, 20–21 April 2010. Retrieved from http://www.dol.gov/ilab/media/events/G20_ministersmeeting/G20-southafrica-brief.pdf

International Labor Office (ILO) (2010b) G20 country briefs: Turkey's response to the crisis. G20 Meeting of Labor and Employment Ministers, Washington, 20–21 April 2010. Retrieved from http://www.dol.gov/ilab/media/events/G20_ministersmeeting/G20-turkey-brief.pdf

Jaradat H (2010) Jordan's economy: crisis challenges and measures. In: Presented at 3rd annual meeting of Middle East and North African senior budget officials, Dubai, UAE, October 31–November 1 2010. Retrieved from http://www.oecd.org/dataoecd/13/46/46382448.pdf

Kehoe T (2010) The current financial crisis in Spain: what should we learn from the great depressions of the twentieth century? In: University of Minnesota and Federal Reserve Bank of Minneapolis, 18th Barcelona Lecture, Barcelona G.S.E. and Banc Sabadell, February 2010

Larbi H (ed) (2009) The financial crisis: impact on the middle east. Quarterly Publication—the World Bank Middle East Department, 1st/2nd quarter 2009

Lin CYY (2011) Leveraging intellectual capital for future competitiveness in Finland, Presentation at Tekes, Helsinki on November 10, 2011.

Lin CYY, Edvinsson L (2011) National intellectual capital: a comparison of 40 countries. Springer Publishing Co, New York

Lyons G (2011) Global overview: fragile west, resilient east, in fragile west, resilient east, global focus-2012. Stand Chartered Glob Res. Retrieved from http://www.privatebank.standard chartered.com/_pdf/en/Global%20Focus%202012.pdf

Mail, Guardian (2012) Business confidence on a steady decline. Retrieved from http://mg.co.za/article/2012-05-03-business-confidence-on-a-steady-decline

Mansur Y (2011) Impact of the financial crisis on Jordan. Retrieved from http://urdunmubdi3.ning.com/forum/topics/impact-of-the-financial-crisis

Nanto DK (2009) The global financial crisis: analysis and policy implications. In: CRS Report for Congress RL34742, Congressional Research Service, pp 7–5700

Ndikumana L, Kamara AB, Chouchane A, Mafusire A (2010) Africa in the wake of the global financial crisis: challenges ahead and the role of the bank. Afr Dev Bank. Retrieved from http://www.afdb.org/fileadmin/uploads/afdb/Documents/Publications/Africa%20in%20the%20wake%20of%20the%20crisis%20-%20English%20-%20Jan%2020_corrected%20March%2023%202010%20A.pdf

OECD (2010) Overview, OECD Economic surveys: South Africa. OECD. Retrieved from http://www.oecd.org/eco/economicsurveyofsouthafrica2010.htm

OECD (2012) Turkey: economic forecast summary. OECD. Retrieved from http://www.oecd.org/turkey/turkey-economicforecastsummarymay2012.htm

Padayachee V (2012) Global economic recession: effects and implications for South Africa at a time of political challenges. Claves de la Economia Mundial, University of KwaZulu-Natal, Durban. Retrieved from http://www2.lse.ac.uk/internationalDevelopment/20thAnniversary Conference/ImpactoftheGlobalFC.pdf in May 2012

Rawdanowicz L (2010) The 2008–009 crisis in Turkey: performance, policy responses and challenges for sustaining the recovery. OECD Economics Department Working Papers, No. 819, OECD Publishing. Retrieved from http://dx.doi.org/10.1787/5km36j7d320s-en

Reavis C (2009) The global financial crisis of 2008-2009: The role of greed, fear and oligarchs. MIT Sloan Manag Case #09-093

Rodrik D (2009) The Turkish economy after the crisis. In: 80th anniversary of the Turkish economics association, Harvard University. Retrieved from http://www.hks.harvard.edu/fs/drodrik/Research%20papers/Turkish%20economy%20after%20the%20crisis.pdf

Rogoff K (2011) In: Javetski B, Koller T Understanding the second great contraction: an interview with Kenneth Rogoff, McKinsey Quarterly. Retrieved from https://www.mckinsey quarterly.com/Economic_Studies/Productivity_Performance/Understanding_the_Second_Great_Contraction_An_interview_with_Kenneth_Rogoff_2871

Rosenberg D (2010) The Israeli economy: after the financial crisis, new challenges. Weeklyblitz. Retrieved from http://www.weeklyblitz.net/680/the-israeli-economy-after-the-financial-crisis

Schwab K (ed) (2011) The global competitiveness report 2011–2012. World Economic Forum, Geneva

State of Israel (2012) Resilience amidst global financial crisis. Ministry of industry trade and labor. Foreign Trade Administration Investment Promotion Center. Retrieved from http://www.investinisrael.gov.il/NR/rdonlyres/270EDC8D-77E2-4363-8B6E-AFC8007B4E88/0/fa in May 2012

Swirski S (2010) Israel and the financial crisis. Presented at the Rosa Luxemburg Forum, Tel Aviv. Retrieved from http://www.adva.org/uploaded/LectureatRosaLuxemburgFoundation.pdf

Togan S (2010) Turkey country report. In: Stiftung B (ed) Managing the crisis. A comparative assessment of economic governance in 14 economies. Bertelsmann Stiftung, Gütersloh 2010. Retrieved from http://www.bertelsmann-transformation-index.de/pdf/Turkey.pdf

Turkish Press (2010) Turkish economy in 2010. Turkish Press. Retrieved from http://www.turkishpress.com/news.asp?id=363124

Warlop SW, Sayed H (2009) Jordan education reforms for knowledge economy: from ERfKE1 to ERfKE2. In: Larbi H (ed) The financial crisis: impact on the middle east. Quarterly Publication, the World Bank Middle East Department, 1st/2nd quarter 2009

Yorukoglu M, Atasoy H (n.d.) The effects of the global financial crisis on the Turkish financial sector. Bank for International Settlements (BIS) paper No. 54. Retrieved from http://www.bis.org/publ/bppdf/bispap54y.pdf

Zini M (2009) Update on the impact of the financial crisis on South Africa. World Bank. Retrieved from http://blogs.worldbank.org/africacan/update-on-the-impact-of-the-financial-crisis-on-south-africa

Author Index

C. Y.-Y. Lin et al., *National Intellectual Capital and the Financial Crisis in Israel, Jordan, South Africa, and Turkey*, SpringerBriefs in Economics,
DOI: 10.1007/978-1-4614-7981-9, © The Author(s) 2014

Subject Index

C. Y.-Y. Lin et al., *National Intellectual Capital and the Financial Crisis in Israel, Jordan, South Africa, and Turkey*, SpringerBriefs in Economics,
DOI: 10.1007/978-1-4614-7981-9, © The Author(s) 2014

Subject Index

MIX
Papier aus verantwortungsvollen Quellen
Paper from responsible sources
FSC® C105338

If you have any concerns about our products,
you can contact us on
ProductSafety@springernature.com

In case Publisher is established outside the EU,
the EU authorized representative is:
Springer Nature Customer Service Center GmbH
Europaplatz 3, 69115 Heidelberg, Germany

Printed by Libri Plureos GmbH
in Hamburg, Germany